the **wild game cookbook**

50 recipes for cooking the different types of feathered, furred and large game, shown in over 200 photographs

ANDY PARLE

southwater

This edition is published by Southwater,
an imprint of Anness Publishing Ltd,
Blaby Road, Wigston,
Leicestershire LE18 4SE;
info@anness.com;

www.southwaterbooks.com; www.annesspublishing.com

If you like the images in this book and would like to investigate using them for publishing, promotions or advertising, please visit our website www.practicalpictures.com for more information.

Publisher: Joanna Lorenz
Editorial Director: Helen Sudell
Executive Editor: Joanne Rippin
Food styling: Fergal Connolly
Props and styling: Liz Hippesley
Food Photography: Craig Robertson
Designer: Nigel Partridge
Additional text: Robert Cuthbert
Additional photography: Jake Eastham

ETHICAL TRADING POLICY
Because of our ongoing ecological investment programme, you, as our customer, can have the pleasure and reassurance of knowing that a tree is being cultivated on your behalf to naturally replace the materials used to make the book you are holding. For further information about this scheme, go to www.annesspublishing.com/trees

NOTES
• Bracketed terms are intended for American readers.
• For all recipes, quantities are given in both metric and imperial measures and, where appropriate, in standard cups and spoons.
• Follow one set of measures, but not a mixture, because they are not interchangeable.
• Standard spoon and cup measures are level. 1 tsp = 5ml, 1 tbsp = 15ml, 1 cup = 250ml/8fl oz.
• Australian standard tablespoons are 20ml. Australian readers should use 3 tsp in place of 1 tbsp for measuring small quantities.
• American pints are 16fl oz/2 cups. American readers should use 20fl oz/2.5 cups in place of 1 pint when measuring liquids.
• Electric oven temperatures in this book are for conventional ovens. When using a fan oven, the temperature will probably need to be reduced by about 10–20°C/20–40°F. As ovens vary, check with your manufacturer's instruction book for guidance.
• The nutritional analysis given for each recipe is calculated per portion (i.e. serving or item), unless otherwise stated. If the recipe gives a range, such as Serves 4–6, then the nutritional analysis will be for the smaller portion size, i.e. 6 servings. The analysis does not include optional ingredients, such as salt added to taste.
• Medium (US large) eggs are used unless otherwise stated.

PUBLISHER'S NOTE
Although the advice and information in this book are believed to be accurate and true at the time of going to press, neither the authors nor the publisher can accept any legal responsibility or liability for any errors or omissions that may have been made nor for any inaccuracies nor for any loss, harm or injury that comes about from following instructions or advice in this book.

Hunting and shooting seasons, laws and regulations concerning the purchase or procurement of quarry species vary from country to country, and state to state, and must be adhered to. In no way are the publishers or authors responsible for any breaches of these laws. Permits\licenses must be obtained in line with the specific regulations of the country you are in, and permission from the landowner should always be obtained. Disposal of offal and waste should be done responsibly and in line with regional health and safety regulations.

Contents

Introduction   4

FEATHERED GAME   6

Roast Teal with Green Peppercorn Sauce and
    Apple Rosti   8
Pan-fried Pigeon and Pease Pudding   10
Pigeon Terrine with Spiced Apricot Chutney   12
Moroccan Pigeon Pie   14
Roast Woodcock Salad with Gooseberry Relish   16
Classic Roast Woodcock with Fried Bread, Game
    Chips and Watercress   18
Pot-roast Grouse with Polenta   20
Grouse Baked in Heather   22
Salmis of Quail   24
Salad of Quail and Truffle Oil   26
Guinea Fowl Normandine   28
Guinea Fowl with Lemon Balm and Mint Butter   29
Roast Partridge with Caramelized Pears   30
Pot-roast Partridge with Grapes and Sherry   32
Cassoulet-style Duck Confit and Beans   34
Sautéed Duck Breast with Jansson's Temptation   36
Roast Duck with Orange an Drambuie   38
Umbrian Roast Pheasant with Spinach Salad   40
Crispy Tarragon Pheasant   41
Norfolk Pheasant Pasty   42
German-style Roast Goose   44
Goose Hash with Fried Egg and Mustard Sauce   46
Rillette of Goose   48
Southern Fried Turkey and Succotash   50
Turkey Schnitzel, Spätzle and Pickled Mushrooms   52

VENISON, BOAR & GOAT   54

Roast Haunch of Roe Deer   56
Venison Heart Braised in Guiness   58
Seared Venison Carpaccio   59
Venison Agrodolce   60
Venison Chilli con Carne   62
Venison Steak with all the Trimmings   64
Daube of Venison   66
Slow-roast Belly of Wild Boar   68
Wild Boar, Chickpea, Saffron and Pepper Stew   69
Sticky Wild Boar Ribs with Boston Baked Beans   70
Wild Boar Hock with Buckwheat Dumplings   72
Crofter's Pie   74
Braised Shoulder of Goat with Anchovy   76
Chunky Goat Moussaka   77
Casserole of Goat with Lettuce and Peas   78

RABBIT, HARE & SQUIRREL   80

Potted Rabbit   82
Polish Hunter's Stew   83
English Rabbit and Game Pie   84
Italian-style Rabbit Casserole   86
Rabbit Salad with Ruby Chard   88
Roast Hare with Beetroot   89
Classic Jugged Hare   90
Game Pâté with Red Onion Marmalade   92
Squirrel Skewers   94
Fricassée of Squirrel and Mustard   95

Index   96

Introduction

For some the idea of taking the life of a bird or animal as part of a sporting endeavour is an uncomfortable one. Others believe that killing animals as and when they are needed for a meal is a much more ethical and natural way of providing food for the table than many intensive farming practices. The birds and animals we're privileged to take for sport can only really be honoured by our subsequent efforts in the kitchen while preparing them for the enjoyment of our friends and family. Whether you pick your pheasants up in the market, go rough shooting with your dog, or control deer as a full-time job, this book offers a wonderful selection of game recipes to make the most of this natural resource.

HANGING GAME

The hanging of game refers to the time allowed between the killing of the bird or animal and the moment when it is ready for cooking. This process is one of the most subjective and divisive issues surrounding the preparation of game dishes. Many people currently writing about the preparation of game still perpetuate the traditional notion that

▼ *Humanity's relationship with dogs is ancient – a symbiotic pairing that almost doubles the enjoyment of hunting.*

▲ *Few other pastimes leave the tired but happy sportsman with some of the tastiest, healthiest foods available.*

game needs to hang for at least a week for it to have any merit or flavour at all. In our view, this simply isn't true, and the recipes in the book reflect this. Tastes have changed and, to this end, we encourage you to lightly hang game birds that are thought to benefit from any hanging time at all. However, do feel free to experiment with a more prolonged hanging time if you prefer meat to have a very strong flavour.

The practice of hanging game is, in blunt terms, to encourage putrefaction or decay. Following the kill, the meat cools: this is to be keenly encouraged and accelerated if at all possible. The meat fibres relax and any fats 'set' and become firmer. This is beneficial, as it allows the all-important game flavour to come through and allows the meat fibres to calm. In general we advocate one to three days in very cool conditions to aid this process; after that, relaxation progresses to the process of decay.

There's no real benefit in hanging pigeon, dove and most types of duck. Indeed duck fat can turn rancid quite quickly in mild temperatures. With each bird species, we've detailed how long we would allow the bird to hang, if at all.

Vitally, all game needs to be kept away from pets while hanging, for obvious reasons. The area should be fly-proof and above all it should be cold, ideally around 7°C/44°F. A slight draught will circulate the air and promote the cooling process.

Consider a pheasant that is hung for just a day. In warm temperatures, the stomach and vent area will quickly turn green, give off a slightly bitter smell and be rendered 'high'; for most people the bird will be completely unsuitable for the table in just hours. On the other hand, a temperature of 5–10°C/40–50°F would make very little difference to the meat in that time. In fact, provided the bird was in perfect condition, without shot having punctured the stomach – the gut in particular – it could probably hang there for three to four days, maybe longer.

Birds should be hung from the neck. Rabbit, squirrel, boar, goat, hare, deer and all other non-feathered game should be hung upside down, by the hind legs. With deer, two weeks in cold conditions seems to result in a tenderness and flavour that is just right; 2°C/35°F is the ideal. Boar can be hung for two or three weeks, again in a very cold area. Another very important factor is the removal of blood from the carcass prior to hanging. There is an enzyme in blood that accelerates decay.

COOKING GAME

The hunter will have to make the best use of whatever he or she happens to shoot, but if you are buying your meat from a game merchant or butchers you will be able to select the bird or animal you cook. Either way, the recipes in the following chapters will supply you with a range of dishes, from the simple to the complex and for any type of game. Notes and tips are given on what to substitute, but remember that most bird recipes can be used for different varieties, and venison and other large game recipes are also fairly interchangeable. For those buying game rather than hunting it, there is plenty of guidance on what to look for and how best to cook it at home. Game dealers and butchers are themselves a hugely underused resource when it comes to the slightly intimidating prospect of choosing suitable game for the pot, so do seek their advice.

The lone pot-hunter, out for a day in the field with a dog and a few pigeons in the bag, may be looking for a change from those flash-fried breast fillets. Rabbit, squirrel and pigeon are good examples of game that can be easily found, shot and cooked in moments with the minimum of fuss but maximum enjoyment. Bag staples like pheasant and partridge blend beautifully with autumn vegetables, while true residents

of the forest, like the woodcock, are perfectly partnered with fungi such as porcini, morels and oyster mushrooms.

EATING GAME

Game is an incredibly healthy source of meat protein, with hardly any natural fat. Because of the free-roaming, grazing nature of many varieties of bird and small game, their diverse diet results in a depth and inimitability of flavour not found in farmed or intensively reared meat, while the various deer species offer a wonderful meat with hardly any waste at all. Birds like partridge, quail and those real prizes, the snipe and the woodcock, can all be cooked in moments, while larger game, venison, boar, or even goat, has a cut for every meal. All you need for a fabulous feast, full of texture and complex flavours, is your field-fresh bird or well-prepared cut of larger game, and one of the many delicious recipes found in this book.

▲ *A lone hunter and his dog rough shooting at sunset among tall grasses full of roosting birds.*

▼ *The recipes in this book include modern takes on classic dishes as well as enterprising new ways to cook game.*

▼ *Terrines, mixed pies, and pâtés are excellent ways for using small amounts of several types of game.*

FEATHERED GAME

Whether you've just taken your first turkey of the season, a brace of pheasant on your last syndicate day, or bagged several wood pigeons from a hide, the following pages offer various recipes, hints and suggestions to help you get the most from your birds. Everyone has a favourite way of cooking their most frequently obtained quarry, but if you have a glut of birds, your priority should be to pluck and draw a large number as efficiently as possible and convert them all into a meal in some way. A roasted bird with all the traditional accompaniments makes a wonderful meal, but sometimes there is only time to whip out the breast fillets and legs and freeze them. Responsible usage is paramount, whether you have a single bird to take home from your game merchant, or several from a day shooting.

◄ *The pleasurable anticipation of a day's shooting with a group of friends is heightened by the thought of the delicious meals your bag will inspire, whether it's a brace of pheasant or a goose.*

Roast Teal with Green Peppercorn Sauce and Apple Rösti

Teal, although small, are full of flavour and can carry robust ingredients such as green peppercorns. The peppercorns are lightly crushed, which helps the heat flood out and brings a warming glow to your cheeks. Served with rösti potatoes and greens, this dish has more than a hint of classical French cooking to it, and would be perfectly partnered with a full-bodied red wine such as a Bordeaux.

Serves 2

2 oven-ready teal
50g/2oz/¼ cup butter
15ml/1tbsp olive oil
4 shallots, peeled and finely chopped
2 garlic cloves, peeled and
    finely chopped
10ml/2 tsp green peppercorns in brine,
    drained and lightly crushed
120ml/4fl oz/½ cup dry white wine
120ml/4fl oz/½ cup Armagnac
275ml/9fl oz/1 generous cup double
    (heavy) cream
15ml/1 tbsp finely chopped parsley
sea salt and ground black pepper
lightly steamed or sautéed greens,
    buttered, to serve

For the apple rösti

675g/1½lb floury potatoes such as
    Maris Piper or King Edward, peeled
75g/3oz/6 tbsp clarified butter, duck
    fat or lard, melted
1 crisp apple, cored and
    coarsely grated
5ml/1 tsp chopped thyme, plus whole
    sprigs to garnish
30ml/2 tbsp olive oil
sea salt and ground black pepper

1 Begin by preparing the apple rösti. Grate the peeled potatoes and sprinkle with plenty of salt.

2 Spread out a clean dish towel and lay the potatoes on top; gather the cloth together and squeeze the potatoes with your hands to remove excess liquid.

3 Transfer the grated potatoes to a bowl and add the clarified butter or fat, grated apple and thyme. Season with pepper and mix well. Preheat the oven to 220°C/425°F/Gas 7.

4 Heat a 20cm/8in frying pan, add the olive oil and heat. Spread the potato and apple mixture evenly in the pan, then press it down.

5 Cook on one side until golden, then turn, pat down and cook until the second side is golden and the potatoes are tender. Remove from the pan and keep warm while you cook the teal.

6 Season each teal with salt and pepper and place a little of the butter inside.

7 Heat an ovenproof frying pan over high heat. Pour the oil into the pan and when hot add the teal and brown on both sides. Brown the breasts too, before finally sitting the birds on their backs. Cook in the hot oven for 10 minutes then remove the teal to a warm serving dish and leave to rest.

8 Put the pan over medium heat and add the remaining butter, shallots, garlic and green peppercorns. Cook, stirring occasionally, until the shallots and garlic have softened.

9 Add the wine and Armagnac and boil rapidly for 1 minute to reduce. Then add the cream and parsley, season and heat thoroughly. Pour any accumulated juices from the resting birds into the sauce and heat again. Cut the apple rösti into wedges and serve with the teal, garnished with thyme, accompanied by the sauce and some buttered greens.

Energy 1828kcal/7575kJ; Protein 30.3g; Carbohydrate 63.8g, of which sugars 13.1g; Fat 152.7g, of which saturates 77.7g; Cholesterol 323mg; Calcium 125mg; Fibre 4.4g; Sodium 641mg

Pan-fried Pigeon and Pease Pudding

Nearly all the pigeon meat worth eating is on the breast, and because pigeon is an inexpensive bird, they tend to be the only part of the bird used in many recipes. The rich taste of pigeon marries well with pease pudding, which is one of Britain's oldest dishes dating back to at least the Middle Ages. Originally the peas would have been wrapped in a cloth and cooked in stock, but here they are cooked loose with a ham bone. It combines well with pigeon, which has a slightly liverish flavour.

Serves 4

450g/1lb/2 cups green or yellow split
  peas, soaked overnight
1 medium onion, diced
1 ham bone, or the rind from a piece
  of smoked bacon
1 thyme sprig
1 parsley sprig
2 mint sprigs
2 bay leaves
50g/2oz/¼ cup butter, plus extra
  for greasing
2 large eggs, beaten
8 pigeon breasts
30ml/2 tbsp vegetable oil
225g/8oz black pudding, sliced into 4
sea salt and ground black pepper
steamed greens, to serve

3 When the peas are soft, remove the herbs and the bone or rind and discard.

4 Drain the peas, reserving the cooking liquor, and purée them in a food processor or with a hand blender, adding the butter, eggs and seasoning as you blend.

8 Place the breasts in the pan, skin side down, and cook for 2–3 minutes, then turn and cook for a further 1–2 minutes. Remove from the pan and keep warm.

1 Drain the soaked peas and place in a large pan. Add the onion, ham bone or rind and enough water to cover the peas. Tie the herb sprigs and bay leaves together with string and add to the pot.

2 Bring to the boil and hold the temperature for 1 minute, then turn the heat down to a gentle simmer. Skim off any scum that has formed and cook for 1 hour until the peas are tender, topping up with more water if necessary.

Cook's tip If there is any pease pudding left over it will keep for up to 4 days in the refrigerator.

5 Transfer the pea mixture to a well-buttered 1.2-litre/2-pint/5-cup heatproof bowl. Butter a sheet of foil and cover the bowl, securing the foil with string or a thick elastic band.

6 Place the bowl in a pan and add water to two-thirds of the height of the bowl. Cover and bring to the boil then reduce the heat and steam the pudding, covered, for 1 hour.

7 When the pease pudding is nearly done, season the pigeon breasts on both sides. Heat a frying pan over medium heat and add the oil.

9 Add the black pudding to the pan and cook for 3 minutes on each side. To serve, spoon the pease pudding on to plates, pile the black pudding and pigeon on top and add steamed greens.

Energy 857kcal/3595kJ; Protein 54.8g; Carbohydrate 73g, of which sugars 3.6g; Fat 40.6g, of which saturates 13.3g; Cholesterol 162mg; Calcium 107mg; Fibre 5.7g; Sodium 919mg

Pigeon Terrine with Spiced Apricot Chutney

A terrine is a great way to start a dinner party as it can be made in advance. Pigeon's gamey flavour makes it ideal for this recipe, but you could substitute other darker game such as hare or grouse. A rich game terrine like this is often accompanied by a sweet relish – in this case a spicy chutney.

Serves 8–10

30ml/2 tbsp vegetable oil
1 small red onion, peeled and diced
2 garlic cloves, peeled and chopped
10ml/1 tsp green peppercorns, crushed
275ml/9fl oz/1 generous cup red wine
8 pigeon breasts, skin removed
675g/1½lb minced (ground) pork
generous pinch each of ground mace,
    ground cinnamon and ground ginger
5ml/1 tsp chopped sage
5ml/1 tsp chopped thyme
12 slices prosciutto
10 prunes, pitted
2 bay leaves
sea salt and ground black pepper

For the chutney
600g/1lb 6oz apricots, chopped
600g/1lb 6oz tomatoes, deseeded and
    roughly chopped
1 medium onion, thinly sliced
4 garlic cloves, thinly sliced
50g/2oz fresh root ginger, grated
2.5ml/½ tsp coriander seeds
2.5ml/½ tsp yellow mustard seeds
5cm/2in cinnamon stick
10ml/2 tsp medium curry powder
275ml/9fl oz/1 generous cup white
    wine vinegar
225g/8oz/1 cup dark muscovado
    (molasses) sugar

1 To make the chutney, place all the ingredients in a wide, heavy pan. Heat gently until simmering, stirring all the time to avoid sticking.

2 Cook for 1 hour or more, until the chutney is thick, then pour into a sterilized jar. The chutney will keep in a cool place for months, but once opened store it in the refrigerator.

3 To make the terrine, heat half the oil in a small pan and fry the onion, garlic and peppercorns until softened. Add the wine and boil to reduce by three-quarters. Leave to cool.

4 Heat the remaining oil in a frying pan over high heat. Season the pigeon breasts and sear for 30 seconds each side. Remove and cool.

5 Place the pork, spices, herbs and cooled wine mixture in a bowl. Season lightly and use your hands to mix all the ingredients thoroughly.

6 Line a 23 x 12 x 7.5cm/9 x 4½ x 3in terrine mould or a 500g/1¼lb loaf tin (pan) with the ham. Start by laying a slice of ham in one end of the mould so that it covers the base and side.

7 Place a second slice of ham in the mould, slightly overlapping the first, and repeat until the base and one side are covered (this should take five slices). Turn the mould and repeat from the other end, hanging the end of each slice over the sides. Arrange the last two slices of ham one at each end. Preheat the oven to 180°C/350°F/Gas 4.

8 One-third fill the terrine with the pork mixture, and top with four of the pigeon breasts, side by side. Fill any gaps around the pigeon with pork before laying a line of the prunes from one end to the other. Once again, fill in any gaps with the pork mixture, and top this with the remaining pigeon.

9 Fill the mould with the rest of the pork mixture. Fold the ham ends over the terrine and lay the bay leaves on top.

10 Cover the terrine with a double layer of foil, put in a deep roasting pan with 2.5cm/1in hot water and place in the oven. After 1 hour, insert a knife into the terrine for 10 seconds, withdraw it and tap it on your wrist. If it is hot, the terrine is cooked. Weight the top of the terrine and leave to cool, then refrigerate for at least 12 hours before slicing and serving with the chutney.

Variations The pigeon can be replaced by any game bird or venison loin, and the chutney can be made with apples, pears, peaches or even pineapple.

Energy 356kcal/1497kJ; Protein 23.4g; Carbohydrate 34.5g, of which sugars 34g; Fat 12.8g, of which saturates 2.9g; Cholesterol 50mg; Calcium 49mg; Fibre 2.6g; Sodium 209mg

Moroccan Pigeon Pie

This is the best way to cook pigeon, because the birds are braised first so that the meat is tender. Pigeon pie, or basteeya, is one of the more elaborate dishes of Morocco. It has travelled well, picking up variations from central Persia, to the Moorish-occupied states of Iberia. A filo pastry pie filled with shredded pigeon, egg, herbs and sugar may sound like a strange concoction, but is delicious.

Serves 4

225g/8oz/1 cup unsalted
   (sweet) butter
1 medium onion, finely chopped
5cm/2in cinnamon stick
generous pinch of saffron strands
2.5ml/½ tsp ground ginger
2.5ml/½ tsp ground coriander
4 plump pigeons
115g/4oz/⅔ cup whole almonds
10ml/2 tsp ground cinnamon, plus
   extra for dusting
15ml/1 tbsp icing (confectioner's)
   sugar, plus extra for dusting
5 large (US extra large) eggs, beaten
bunch of fresh coriander (cilantro),
   finely chopped
bunch of parsley, finely chopped
12 sheets filo pastry
sea salt and ground black pepper

1 In a pan just big enough to hold the four pigeons, put 50g/2oz/¼ cup of the butter, the onion and spices and place the pigeons on top. Add water to just cover the birds, along with a generous pinch of salt and lots of black pepper.

2 Bring the water to a simmer, cover the pan and braise for 35–45 minutes, until the meat is tender and falling off the bones. Remove the pigeons from the pan, drain and leave to cool. Discard the cinnamon stick and leave the cooking liquid to bubble until reduced to a syrup.

3 When the pigeons have cooled enough to handle, strip the meat from the bones, chop roughly and set aside. Discard the carcasses. Preheat the oven to 180°C/350°F/Gas 4.

4 Melt 25g/1oz of the butter in a pan and fry the almonds. When they are golden, add the ground cinnamon and icing sugar and mix well. Remove the mixture from the pan and leave to cool, then chop roughly.

5 Add the beaten eggs and chopped herbs to the reduced pigeon stock and cook, stirring, for 5 minutes until the eggs are scrambled, then set aside.

6 Melt the remaining butter in a pan and generously brush a 23cm/9in cake tin (pan) with some of it.

Variation The pigeons can be replaced with almost any small game birds, such as teal, mallard, quail, guinea fowl and even pheasant.

7 Lay a sheet of filo pastry in the bottom of the tin, brush with butter and lay a second sheet half in the tin and half hanging over the edge; brush again and place a third filo sheet 60 degrees further around the tin, overlapping the other. Repeat with five further sheets.

8 Sprinkle cinnamon and icing sugar in the base of the tin, pour in half the egg mixture and spread it out. Layer half the almonds, all the meat, the remaining almonds and the rest of the eggs. Butter a sheet of filo, fold it in half, place it on top of the pie and dust with more cinnamon and icing sugar.

9 Fold the overlapping pastry edges over the pie and press down. Butter the two remaining sheets of filo together, lay them over the pie and tuck the edges down to create a smooth top. Brush with butter and bake for 45 minutes, until golden. Remove from the oven, dust with icing sugar and cinnamon and serve immediately.

Energy 980kcal/4066kJ; Protein 44.2g; Carbohydrate 19.2g, of which sugars 2.8g; Fat 81.5g, of which saturates 33.7g; Cholesterol 384mg; Calcium 204mg; Fibre 3.9g; Sodium 632mg

Roast Woodcock Salad with Gooseberry Relish

The gooseberry season is all too short, so make the most of it by preserving these delicious berries. This simple preserve will keep in the refrigerator for several months, so make a big batch as it goes well with oily fish and cheese as well as many game dishes. This warm salad of woodcock, with bitter leaves and crunchy hazelnuts to balance the sweet-sour relish, makes a good first course.

Serves 2

15ml/1 tbsp vegetable oil
1 woodcock, drawn and cleaned
25g/1oz/2 tbsp butter
2 handfuls mixed leaves, such as
  chicory (Belgian endive), frisée
  and radicchio
sea salt and ground black pepper

For the gooseberry relish
250g/9oz/2 cups gooseberries
50g/2oz/¼ cup caster
  (superfine) sugar
5ml/1 tsp lemon juice
3 cloves

For the dressing
12 hazelnuts, toasted in the oven,
  skins rubbed off, lightly crushed
45ml/3 tbsp extra virgin olive oil
15ml/1 tbsp red wine vinegar
5ml/1 tsp oregano, chopped
sea salt and ground black pepper

1 First make the gooseberry relish. Place the berries, sugar, lemon juice and cloves in a pan, cover and heat gently for 8–10 minutes, stirring occasionally.

Cook's tip If you have more gooseberries than you need for this dish, increase the other relish ingredients accordingly to use up all the fruit. Freeze what you don't use in small batches, to be defrosted as needed to accompany most roasted game birds.

2 Once the fruit has begun to soften, increase the heat and cook the relish for 2 minutes, then remove from the heat and keep warm. Preheat the oven to 220°C/425°F/Gas 7.

3 Make the dressing by putting the hazelnuts, olive oil, vinegar and oregano into a jar. Season with salt and pepper, close the lid and shake vigorously.

4 Heat a small ovenproof frying pan over medium heat and add the oil. Season the woodcock with salt and pepper and place in the pan, turning it to brown on all sides.

5 Smear the woodcock with the rest of the butter and place in the oven for 10 minutes. Baste the bird halfway through the cooking time. Remove from the oven and leave to rest in a warm place.

6 To assemble the salad, remove the breasts and legs from the carcass and slice each breast into three, divide the leaves between two bowls and arrange the meat on top. Spoon over the hazelnut dressing and add a spoonful of the gooseberry relish on the side.

Variation This salad would be suited to all the small game birds, as well as to wild boar and venison.

Energy 622kcal/2585kJ; Protein 18.4g; Carbohydrate 31.5g, of which sugars 31.3g; Fat 47.9g, of which saturates 10.3g; Cholesterol 29mg; Calcium 90mg; Fibre 4.3g; Sodium 155mg

Classic Roast Woodcock with Fried Bread, Game Chips and Watercress

The traditional way to prepare woodcock is to pluck it, remove the gizzard and truss it with its beak, before roasting it whole. The innards are then removed and served spread on fried bread. This is a dish that conjures images of Edwardian gentlemen quaffing red wine poured from crystal decanters in the club dining rooms and restaurants of London; it has to be tried at least once.

Serves 4

4 woodcock, gizzards removed
115g/4oz/½ cup butter
4 thyme sprigs
4 rashers (strips) streaky (fatty) bacon,
   cut in half crossways
15ml/1 tbsp vegetable oil
4 thick slices white bread,
   crusts removed
4 bunches peppery watercress
275ml/9fl oz/1 generous cup red wine
sea salt and ground black pepper
redcurrant jelly, to serve

For the game chips
2 large floury potatoes, peeled
vegetable oil, for frying

1 Truss each bird by spearing the beak through one drumstick, over the breastbone and through the other drumstick. (Alternatively tuck the head under the bird.) Rub 25g/1oz/2 tbsp of the butter over each bird, season well with salt and pepper, place one sprig of thyme on each crown and cover with two half rashers of bacon, crossed.

2 For the game chips, slice the potatoes thinly with a mandolin or vegetable peeler and soak in water for 10 minutes.

3 Preheat the oven to 220°C/425°F/ Gas 7. Place the oil in an ovenproof pan and put in the oven to heat up. Arrange the birds in the hot pan and roast for 5 minutes. Baste with the pan juices and cook for a further 4 minutes.

4 Remove the bacon and thyme from the birds, reserving them for later. Baste again and cook for a further 5 minutes to crisp the skin. Remove from the oven and leave to rest in the pan.

5 Meanwhile, heat a deep fat fryer to 150°C/300°F. Drain the potatoes, pat dry with kitchen paper and place in the fryer, stirring the oil as you do so to separate the potato slices.

6 Fry the game chips for 5 minutes until golden, then remove from the fryer and transfer to kitchen paper to remove any excess oil. Season with salt.

Cook's tip Some people extend their enjoyment of this classic dish by splitting the head and beak so that the brain can be scooped out and eaten.

Variation Use crisps (US potato chips) instead of making game chips.

7 Use the fat from the pan containing the woodcock to fry the bread slices on both sides; if there isn't enough, supplement it with some vegetable oil or butter. Keep the fried bread warm.

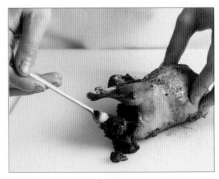

8 Slit the rear of each bird and carefully insert a spoon, rotating it around the inner cavity of the woodcock to draw out the innards.

9 Chop the reserved bacon rashers and add to the roasting pan along with the innards and thyme, crushing them into the buttery juices. Fry for 2 minutes, then divide the mixture into four and spread on to the slices of fried bread. Add the wine to the pan, and boil rapidly to create a thin gravy.

10 To serve, place the woodcock on the bread and innards, and accompany with the game chips, a good handful of watercress and some redcurrant jelly.

Energy 629kcal/2631kJ; Protein 30.7g; Carbohydrate 41.1g, of which sugars 2.9g; Fat 34.1g, of which saturates 3.4g; Cholesterol 8mg; Calcium 122mg; Fibre 2.1g; Sodium 531mg

Pot-roast Grouse with Polenta

If you bag an older bird it may well result in a dry and tough meal, but pot-roasting in plenty of liquid helps the meat stay moist and flavoursome. In this case, rich red wine and raisins give a taste typical of southern Europe, with Moorish influences. The grouse are served with soft polenta enriched with Parmesan cheese, butter and sage to add an Italian feel. Serve with buttered cabbage or green beans.

Serves 4

45ml/3 tbsp olive oil
4 grouse, drawn and cleaned
1 medium onion, peeled and diced
2 medium carrots, peeled and diced
1 stick of celery, diced
4 garlic cloves, peeled and sliced
2.5cm/1in cinnamon stick
1 bay leaf
1 thyme sprig
1 bottle rich Italian red wine such as
  Barolo or Chianti
50g/2oz/⅓ cup raisins
50g/2oz/⅓ cup pine kernels, toasted
30ml/2 tbsp marjoram or oregano
sea salt and ground black pepper

For the polenta
175g/6oz/1½ cups cornmeal
50g/2oz Parmesan cheese, grated
50g/2oz/¼ cup butter
12 sage leaves, shredded

1 Put the oil in a casserole just large enough to hold the birds and warm over medium heat. Season the grouse and put them in the pan one at a time, turning them to brown on all sides, then set aside. Preheat the oven to 180°C/350°F/Gas 4.

Variations If you are unsure about polenta simply replace it with mashed potatoes flavoured with the cheese, butter and sage. Older pheasants would be a perfect alternative to the grouse.

2 Add the onion, carrots, celery and garlic to the oil in the casserole, reduce the heat to low and cook gently for 12–15 minutes until softened and golden. Stir in the cinnamon stick, bay leaf and thyme.

3 Return the grouse to the pan, pour the wine over and around the birds and sprinkle the raisins over the top.

4 Bring the contents of the pan to a simmer, season with salt and pepper, cover and place in the oven. Cook for 45 minutes.

5 Meanwhile, to make the polenta, pour 1.2 litres/2 pints/5 cups water into a heavy pan, salt well and bring to the boil. Pour the cornmeal into the pan in a steady stream, whisking constantly as you do so.

6 As it thickens, reduce the heat, add 150ml/¼ pint/⅔ cup boiling water and keep stirring with a wooden spoon.

7 Continue to cook for 40–45 minutes over gentle heat, by which time the polenta should be smooth and creamy. Add a little more hot water if it begins to get too thick.

8 When cooked, remove the grouse from the oven. Add the pine kernels and marjoram or oregano, and a little water if the liquid is low, and return to the oven for a further 15 minutes.

9 When you are ready to serve the grouse, add the Parmesan cheese, butter and sage to the polenta, and season with plenty of black pepper and additional salt, if needed.

10 Pile some of the polenta on to each plate and top with a grouse, with plenty of sauce spooned over the top. If you wish, shallow-fry a few whole sage leaves and sprinkle them over the dish as a flavoursome garnish.

Energy 748kcal/3131kJ; Protein 75.4g; Carbohydrate 17.7g, of which sugars 16.3g; Fat 29.4g, of which saturates 4.6g; Cholesterol 0mg; Calcium 118mg; Fibre 2.5g; Sodium 264mg

Grouse Baked in Heather

Grouse are often found feeding on the young tender shoots of heather, which gives the birds a very distinctive flavour. The heather can also be used to cook them: here the bird is surrounded with sprigs of heather in a sealed pot to keep it moist and juicy. Grouse are hunted on the moors of the English and Scottish borders, and this is reflected in the accompaniment of black pudding and pan haggerty – a traditional potato cake layered with cheese and onion, from the far north of England.

Serves 2

25g/1oz/2 tbsp butter
2 grouse, drawn and cleaned
large handful of heather
225g/8oz/2 cups plain (all-purpose)
   flour mixed to a thick paste with a
   little water
sea salt and ground black pepper

For the pan haggerty
350g/12oz potatoes, peeled and sliced
   as thinly as possible
50g/2oz/¼ cup butter, melted
2 medium onions, thinly sliced
75g/3oz mature (sharp) cheese such
   as Cheddar or Lancashire, grated
5ml/1 tsp chopped parsley
4 thick slices black pudding (find one
   made with barley if possible)

1 Preheat the oven to 220°C/425°F/ Gas 7. Place half the butter inside each grouse and season them inside and out.

2 Prepare a cooking pot with a tight-fitting lid by lining the base with moist heather. Place the grouse on top of the heather. Tuck heather around the sides and over the birds so they are completely covered.

Variation This method will work well with wild duck. If you do not have any heather you can replace it with some moistened straw or hay.

3 Spread the flour paste around the rim of the pot and press the lid down firmly to create a seal before putting it in the oven and baking for 1 hour.

4 While the grouse are cooking, begin the pan haggerty. Rinse the sliced potatoes in cold water, drain and pat dry. Put the potatoes in a bowl, add the butter, season with salt and pepper and mix to coat the slices evenly.

5 Line the bottom of an ovenproof frying pan with overlapping slices of potato, sprinkle over half of the onion slices, half the grated cheese and half the chopped parsley.

6 Add a second layer of potato slices to the pan, then the remaining onion, cheese and parsley and finish with a layer of potato. Place the pan over medium heat and warm through to start the cooking.

7 Cover with baking parchment or foil, and place in the oven for 30 minutes.

8 After 30 minutes, arrange the slices of black pudding on top and continue to cook, uncovered, for 10 minutes.

9 When you are ready to eat, break the seal of the pot of grouse by running the tip of a knife around the rim. Remove the birds, wipe away any adhering heather with damp kitchen paper, cut the legs and breast from the bones and serve with the pan haggerty.

Energy 1379kcal/5749kJ; Protein 107.6g; Carbohydrate 50g, of which sugars 10.9g; Fat 83.6g, of which saturates 39.5g; Cholesterol 825mg; Calcium 491mg; Fibre 4g; Sodium 1251mg

Salmis of Quail

The salmis is a classic dish of French cuisine, often made using game birds. The word relates to meat that has been quickly cooked and then reheated in a rich sauce. It is a complex dish for which you must first make a thickened stock, but the end result has an intensity of flavour that is worth the effort.

Serves 2

For the stock
1kg/2¼lb chicken or game bird
   bones, chopped
1 medium onion, cut into 4 wedges
2 medium carrots, cut in half
   lengthways
1 celery stick
4 garlic cloves, unpeeled
30ml/2 tbsp vegetable oil
1 thyme sprig
1 bay leaf
15ml/1 tbsp tomato purée (paste)
25g/1oz/2 tbsp butter, softened
25g/1oz/2 tbsp plain (all-purpose) flour
braised red cabbage and Sarladaise
   potatoes (see Cook's tip), to serve

For the salmis
4 quail, drawn, livers reserved
75g/3oz/6 tbsp butter
1 medium carrot, diced
4 shallots, finely chopped
2 garlic cloves, finely chopped
1 thyme sprig
1 bay leaf
150ml/¼ pint/⅔ cup dry white wine
12 button (white) mushrooms,
   quartered
150ml/¼ pint/⅔ cup cognac or brandy
sea salt and ground black pepper

1 To make the stock, preheat the oven to 220°C/425°F/Gas 7. Place the bones, onion, carrots, celery and garlic in a roasting pan, drizzle with oil and roast in the hot oven for 15 minutes.

2 Remove the roasting pan from the oven and turn the bones and vegetables over. Repeat, turning the ingredients every 15 minutes, until the bones and vegetables are well browned.

3 Add the thyme, bay leaf and tomato purée to the roasting pan with 1 litre/1¾ pints/4 cups water. Bring to the boil over medium heat, scraping the pan to release any residue, then pour the contents of the pan into a stockpot.

4 Cover the contents of the stockpot with twice the volume of water, bring to the boil, skim and reduce the heat. Simmer for 4 hours. Strain the stock into a second pan and place over high heat; boil until the liquid is reduced to 600ml/ 1 pint/2½ cups.

5 Knead the butter and flour together to make a smooth paste and gradually whisk into the liquid a little at a time; cook for 10 minutes until the stock has thickened. Strain again and reserve.

6 To make the salmis, rub the quail with 50g/2oz/¼ cup of the butter and season with salt and pepper. Put the birds in an ovenproof frying pan and roast in the hot oven for 5 minutes.

7 Remove the birds from the oven, and cut the breasts and legs away from the bones. Place in an ovenproof dish.

8 Chop the bones and the reserved livers and put them into a pan with the carrot, shallot and garlic. Fry until they begin to caramelize.

9 Add the herbs and wine to the pan, boil until the wine has nearly evaporated then add the thickened stock. Bring to a simmer and cook for 20 minutes.

10 Meanwhile, in a separate pan, sauté the mushrooms in the remaining butter. When the mushrooms are cooked, pour the cognac into the pan and flame to burn off the alcohol. Spoon the mushrooms over the quail.

Energy 612kcal/2547kJ; Protein 31.7g; Carbohydrate 15.6g, of which sugars 5.2g; Fat 24.6g, of which saturates 6.9g; Cholesterol 29mg; Calcium 62mg; Fibre 2g; Sodium 219mg

11 To finish the dish, strain the sauce, pressing out all the juices from the bones and vegetables. Pour over the quail and transfer to the oven, covered with a sheet of baking parchment, for 6–8 minutes until the meat is completely cooked. Serve with Sarladaise potatoes (see Cook's tip) and braised red cabbage.

Cook's tip To make Sarladaise potatoes, peel and very thinly slice 4 medium potatoes. Place in a bowl. Pour over 50g/2oz/4 tbsp melted duck fat, add chopped rosemary and plenty of salt and pepper. Layer the potatoes in an ovenproof dish and bake at 180°C/350°F/Gas 4 for 45 minutes, until the potatoes are soft and golden.

Salad of Quail and Truffle Oil

The delicate flavour of quail lends itself to a light, late summer salad.
Served with creamy soft-boiled quail eggs and crisp, tart apples,
they make an elegant first course or light lunch.

Serves 4

8 quail's eggs
1 egg yolk
15ml/1 tbsp white wine vinegar
120ml/4fl oz/½ cup olive oil
30ml/2 tbsp white truffle oil
15ml/1 tbsp apple juice
15ml/1 tbsp finely chopped chives
12 baby potatoes, scrubbed, boiled,
  cooled and diced
30ml/2 tbsp vegetable oil
4 oven-ready quail
2 Little Gem (Bibb) lettuces
2 crisp eating apples, cored and
  thinly sliced
sea salt and ground black pepper
fresh chives, chopped, to garnish

1 Bring a small pan of water to the boil,
place the quail's eggs in it and boil for
2 minutes 10 seconds. Cool under cold
running water. Carefully peel the eggs
and reserve. Preheat the oven to
220°C/425°F/Gas 7.

2 To make the dressing, place the egg
yolk and vinegar in a large bowl. Gently
whisk them together and gradually add
the olive oil in a steady trickle, whisking
all the time until it is all incorporated and
a thick mayonnaise has formed.

3 Whisk the truffle oil, apple juice and
chives into the mayonnaise, and season
to taste with salt and pepper.

4 Fold the diced cooked potatoes into
the mayonnaise and set aside.

5 Heat the vegetable oil in a frying pan
over high heat. Season the quail with
salt and pepper and place in the pan,
turning to brown quickly on all sides.
Put the pan in the oven and roast for
6–8 minutes, depending on size.

6 Allow the quail to rest and cool. Take
the meat off the bone and roughly shred it
with your fingers. Divide the lettuce leaves,
quail's eggs and apple slices among four
bowls, add the potato mayonnaise and
top with the shredded quail meat.

Energy 364kcal/1505kJ; Protein 4.6g; Carbohydrate 9.3g, of which sugars 5.6g; Fat 34.6g, of which saturates 5.5g;
Cholesterol 146mg; Calcium 31mg; Fibre 1.3g; Sodium 42mg

Guinea Fowl Normandine

These birds are usually only available through game merchants, outside of their native Africa. The flesh of guinea fowl is delicious, and works well in this adaption of a pork dish from northern France, a combination of orchard fruits, Calvados and crème fraîche that is also perfect for game.

Serves 4

1 large guinea fowl, jointed
50g/2oz/¼ cup butter
115g/4oz smoked streaky (fatty)
   bacon, diced
1 medium onion, diced
4 garlic cloves, peeled and sliced
275ml/9fl oz/1 generous cup medium
   (hard) cider
2 apples, cored and diced
75ml/2½fl oz/⅓ cup Calvados
250g/9oz/1 cup crème fraîche
8 sage leaves, finely torn
sea salt and ground black pepper
mashed potatoes and green beans,
   to serve

2 Put the bacon in the pan and fry gently to render its fat. As the fat runs and the bacon begins to brown, add the onion and garlic and sweat them gently in the fat until softened, but without colouring.

1 Season the guinea fowl pieces with salt and pepper. Heat a large heavy pan over medium heat and melt the butter.

3 Increase the heat, add the pieces of guinea fowl and cook, turning occasionally, to brown on all sides.

4 Add the cider to the pan and bring to the boil. Reduce the heat and cover with baking parchment or foil. Simmer gently for 25–30 minutes.

5 Remove the baking parchment, stir in the apples and Calvados and cook for a further 5 minutes to soften the apples.

6 Remove the guinea fowl to a serving dish. Finish the sauce by whisking in the crème fraîche and sage. Return to a gentle simmer (do not allow to boil), season to taste and pour the sauce over the bird. Serve immediately with mashed potatoes and green beans.

Energy 640kcal/2658kJ; Protein 35.3g; Carbohydrate 11.2g, of which sugars 10.6g; Fat 44.3g, of which saturates 23.5g; Cholesterol 319mg; Calcium 80mg; Fibre 1.4g; Sodium 451mg

Guinea Fowl with Lemon Balm and Mint Butter

Early summer brings produce in abundance that just begs to be eaten together. First crop new potatoes and sensual asparagus can turn any plate into a gastronomic delight, and this simple roast guinea fowl, oozing with herbs and lemon balm butter, is an excellent accompaniment for them.

Serves 4

175g/6oz/¾ cup butter, softened
2 good handfuls lemon balm
1 handful mint
2 garlic cloves, peeled and chopped
1 lemon, rind removed, quartered
1 oven-ready guinea fowl
675g/1½lb Jersey Royal potatoes
1 bunch asparagus (20 spears),
    trimmed
sea salt and ground black pepper

1 Preheat the oven to 220°C/425°F/ Gas 7. Place the butter, herbs, garlic and lemon rind in a food processor and blitz until smooth. Smear the butter mixture over the guinea fowl inside and out and season well. Tuck the lemon quarters in the cavity, put the bird into a large roasting pan and place in the hot oven for 12–15 minutes.

2 Baste the guinea fowl with the melted butter, reduce the oven temperature to 180°C/350°F/Gas 4 and cook for a further 30 minutes. Baste occasionally.

3 Meanwhile, bring a pan of salted water to the boil, put the potatoes in and boil for 12 minutes or until tender. When the potatoes are nearly cooked add the asparagus to the pan and cook for 2 minutes until just tender. Drain the vegetables and keep warm.

4 Once everything is ready, carve the guinea fowl and reserve on a warmed serving plate. Squeeze the lemon quarters into the roasting pan, add the potatoes and asparagus and gently toss to coat the vegetables in the herby juices before serving.

Energy 547kcal/2282kJ; Protein 33.8g; Carbohydrate 28.5g, of which sugars 3.4g; Fat 33.8g, of which saturates 17.9g; Cholesterol 288mg; Calcium 83mg; Fibre 3.2g; Sodium 279mg

Roast Partridge with Caramelized Pears

In this recipe the gaminess of partridge plays against the subtle sweetness and soft texture of pears. To round off the dish the birds are served with clapshot potatoes (so called because the mashed potatoes contain little pieces of swede as if having been fired from a cartridge). There are two main varieties of partridge – the English grey leg, which is slightly smaller, and the French red leg. This recipe uses the English variety but if you have French add a couple of minutes to the cooking time.

Serves 4

75g/3oz/6 tbsp butter, softened
4 oven-ready partridges
30ml/2 tbsp olive oil
3 large pears, quartered and cored
5ml/1 tsp honey
8 sage leaves
150ml/5fl oz/⅔ cup perry or (hard) cider
sea salt and ground black pepper

For the clapshot potatoes

1.2kg/2½lb floury potatoes, peeled
75g/3oz/6 tbsp butter
350g/12oz swede (rutabaga), diced
12–16 sage leaves, finely shredded
sea salt and ground black pepper

1 Preheat the oven to 200°C/400°F/ Gas 6. Divide 25g/1oz/2 tbsp of the butter into four and place a knob in the cavity of each bird. Season inside and outside with plenty of salt and pepper.

2 Heat a large ovenproof frying pan over medium heat and add the oil. Place the birds in the pan and brown evenly on all sides. Lean them against the side of the pan so they are sitting on their breastbones and place in the hot oven for 10 minutes.

3 Remove from the oven, roll the birds in the pan juices and remove to a warmed dish to rest and keep warm. Set aside the pan with its juices.

4 Meanwhile, make the clapshot potatoes. Place the potatoes in a large pan of salted water, bring to the boil, reduce the heat and simmer for 12–15 minutes, until just tender but not breaking up.

5 While the potatoes are cooking, melt the butter in a frying pan, add the diced swede, season and fry gently, turning occasionally, until softened. Add the shredded sage leaves and cook for 1 minute in the butter.

6 When the potatoes are cooked, drain them in a colander, return to the pan and mash until smooth.

7 Add the mashed potato to the swede, folding the contents of the pan together. Keep warm while you cook the pears.

Variation Try this recipe with quail instead of partridge. It would also work well with jointed rabbit.

8 Melt the remaining butter in the pan used for the partridges, and fry the pears gently on all sides until golden, Add the sage and honey.

9 Turn the heat up, add the perry or cider and bubble vigorously to reduce. Season, then return the birds to the pan along with any gathered juices. Serve with the clapshot potatoes.

Energy 1126kcal/4730kJ; Protein 127.2g; Carbohydrate 64.9g, of which sugars 20.4g; Fat 40.3g, of which saturates 16.5g; Cholesterol 43mg; Calcium 237mg; Fibre 7.1g; Sodium 523mg

Pot-roast Partridge with Grapes and Sherry

Pot-roasting is a favourite method of cooking game, as it keeps the meat nice and moist. In this Spanish-influenced dish, the addition of intense raisin-flavoured sherry produces a deep, rich gravy. Partnered with broad beans fried with Serrano ham and some simply boiled rice, it is a dish fit for 'el rey'.

Serves 4

4 oven-ready partridges
45ml/3 tbsp olive oil
2 large onions, finely diced
2 medium carrots, finely diced
1 celery stick, finely chopped
4 garlic cloves, thinly sliced
200ml/7fl oz/scant 1 cup Pedro
   Ximénez sherry
200ml/7fl oz/scant 1 cup good chicken
   or game bird stock
1 bay leaf
15 seedless white grapes, halved
15 seedless black grapes, halved
15ml/1 tbsp chopped marjoram
sea salt and ground black pepper
boiled rice, to serve

For the broad beans and ham
30ml/2 tbsp olive oil
115g/4oz Serrano ham, cut into dice
   or strips
1 medium onion, finely diced
350g/12oz/2½ cups fresh podded
   broad (fava) beans, simmered for
   3 minutes in unsalted water, or
   frozen baby broad beans, defrosted

1 Season the partridges with salt and pepper. Heat a casserole over medium heat, add the oil and warm.

2 Place the birds in the dish and fry gently on all sides to brown, then remove and reserve. Preheat the oven to 180°C/350°F/Gas 4.

3 Put the onion and carrot in the dish and cook, stirring, for 8–10 minutes until tender. Add the celery and garlic and continue to cook until all the vegetables are softened.

4 Return the birds to the dish, increase the heat and add the sherry, allowing it to boil briefly. Add the stock and bay leaf, bring to a simmer, cover and place in the oven for 15–18 minutes, depending on the size of the partridges. (Test by prising a leg away from the body; the flesh at the hip joint should be just cooked through.)

Variation Try this recipe with wood pigeon (12 minutes in the oven) or pheasant (30–35 minutes).

5 Remove the birds from the pan once more, add the grapes and marjoram to the juices and simmer lightly until the stock is rich and the grapes soft. Correct the seasoning. Put the birds back in the pan and replace the lid to keep them warm.

6 To make the broad beans and ham, warm the oil in a frying pan, add the ham and cook gently to render the fat and infuse the oil with its aroma.

7 Add the onion and cook until translucent (about 8–10 minutes) before adding the cooked beans and some salt and pepper.

8 Cook the beans, ham and onion together gently for 5 minutes, stirring occasionally. Then serve immediately with the partridge and boiled rice.

Cook's tip If the broad beans are large you might want to skin them. After cooking, run under cold water, then pop out of their skins.

Energy 932kcal/3908kJ; Protein 133.4g; Carbohydrate 17.4g, of which sugars 9.4g; Fat 30.9g, of which saturates 7.3g; Cholesterol 17mg; Calcium 219mg; Fibre 5.2g; Sodium 695mg

Cassoulet-style Duck Confit and Beans

Not so long ago the preservation of seasonal foods for the hard times of winter was common practice. Cassoulet is a dish made with preserved duck or goose, salted and cooked in its own fat and originally stored in earthenware pots in the cellar. You will need to start at least one day in advance.

Serves 6

115g/4oz/½ cup duck fat
1 medium onion, diced
2 medium carrots, diced
2 celery sticks, chopped
6 garlic cloves: 4 sliced, 2 crushed
6 tomatoes, chopped
275ml/9fl oz/1 generous cup dry
    white wine
2 bay leaves
2 thyme sprigs
115g/4oz/2 cups white breadcrumbs
15ml/1 tbsp chopped parsley
sea salt and ground black pepper

For the confit
2 plump wild ducks, plucked and
    cleaned, legs cut from carcass,
    crown cut off and split in half
50g/2oz/¼ cup rock salt
2 bay leaves
1 thyme sprig
5ml/1 tsp crushed black pepper
2.5ml/½ tsp crushed juniper berries
1kg/2¼lb/4½ cups duck, goose, pork
    or beef fat, or a mixture

For the beans
500g/1¼lb/3 cups dried white beans,
    soaked overnight in cold water
400g/14oz pork belly, in one piece
250g/9oz fresh garlic sausage

1 To make the confit, mix all the ingredients except the fat in a shallow dish, coating the duck evenly with salt. Leave in a cool place for 12–24 hours.

2 Wipe the duck clean of the herby salt, rinse briefly in cold water and pat dry. Preheat the oven to 160°C/325°F/Gas 3.

3 Melt the fat in a roasting pan and add the duck pieces; they should be fully covered by the fat. Warm gently on the stove, then cover loosely with baking parchment and put into the oven for approximately 1 hour. The meat should be nearly falling off the bones. The confit can be cooked in advance and kept in the refrigerator, still covered by its fat.

4 To prepare the beans, drain off the soaking water and place them in a pan with fresh water to cover. Bring to the boil and cook for 2 minutes. Drain and return to the pan with the pork, sausage and water to cover, bring to a simmer, cover and cook gently for 15 minutes.

5 Remove the sausage and reserve, then cook the beans for a further 45–60 minutes. Reserve the beans in their cooking liquor. This can also be done in advance.

6 Assemble the cassoulet at least 1 hour before serving. Preheat the oven to 200°C/400°F/Gas 6. In a large, wide casserole, heat 75g/3oz/6 tbsp of the duck fat. Add the onion, carrot, celery and sliced garlic cloves and cook over a medium heat until softened. Add the tomatoes and wine and boil briefly before removing from the heat.

7 Put half the cooked beans into the bottom of the dish, reserving the cooking liquor, and mix with the vegetables. Cover with the meat, evenly dispersed, and add the bay leaves and thyme. Cover with the remaining beans. Add enough of the reserved bean stock to just come to the surface. Heat gently.

8 Mix the breadcrumbs, crushed garlic and parsley with some seasoning and the remaining fat. Sprinkle over the cassoulet and transfer the dish to the oven. Cook for 30–45 minutes, adding bean stock at the edge if the dish starts to look a little too dry. Serve when the topping is crispy and golden.

Energy 861kcal/3601kJ; Protein 45.4g; Carbohydrate 56.1g, of which sugars 6.8g; Fat 49g, of which saturates 18.3g; Cholesterol 141mg; Calcium 141mg; Fibre 14.8g; Sodium 306mg

Sautéed Duck Breast with Jansson's Temptation

Hunting is a popular sport in Sweden, although grouse is more commonly shot here than duck. As in most countries, however, wild duck is widely available from good butchers and game merchants. Jansson's temptation is a Swedish dish eaten mainly in the winter months, which makes it the perfect accompaniment to game. It is high in carbohydrates and calories: good news if you live in a cold climate, but this is a lighter version, which uses salted anchovies rather than salted herring.

Serves 4

1.2 litres/2 pints/5 cups double
   (heavy) cream
600ml/1 pint/2½ cups milk
2 garlic cloves, peeled and
   thinly sliced
1 medium onion, thinly sliced
6 good gratings of fresh nutmeg
1.3kg/3lb floury potatoes such as
   Maris Piper or King Edward, peeled,
   coarsely grated and squeezed in a
   towel to remove excess water
12 salted anchovy fillets, chopped
30ml/2 tbsp dill, roughly chopped
4 duck breasts
15ml/1 tbsp vegetable oil
50g/2oz/½ cup butter
20–24 raspberries
15ml/1 tbsp raspberry or cider vinegar
sea salt and ground black pepper
crisp green leaf salad, to serve (see
   Cook's tip)

1 Place the cream, milk, garlic, sliced onion and nutmeg in a large heavy pan and bring to a simmer over medium heat. Preheat the oven to 200°C/400°F/Gas 6.

2 Once the cream mixture is simmering, stir in the grated, squeezed potato. Season and cook gently, stirring, for 5 minutes, until the mixture has thickened and the potatoes are just tender to the touch.

3 Add the anchovies and dill to the potato and cream and mix well.

4 Pour the mixture into a 30 x 20 x 7.5cm/12 x 8 x 3in baking dish and place in the oven for 20–30 minutes, until thick and golden on top.

5 Meanwhile, warm a frying pan over medium heat. Season the duck breasts. Add the oil to the pan and place the duck skin-side down in the pan.

6 Allow the duck breasts to cook for 5 minutes, then turn and cook on the other side for 2 minutes. Remove the breasts from the pan and leave to rest in a warm place.

7 Add the butter to the pan, and when it is foaming add the raspberries. Cook for 1 minute then add the vinegar and allow it to bubble.

8 To serve, slice each duck breast across into three pieces, drizzle over the vinegar, butter and raspberry mixture and add a generous spoonful of Jansson's Temptation.

Cook's tip Try serving this dish with a crisp leaf salad, tossed with capers, sliced sweet pickled gherkins and thinly sliced red onion.

Energy 1938kcal/8036kJ; Protein 46.5g; Carbohydrate 69.7g, of which sugars 21.3g; Fat 185.4g, of which saturates 100.5g; Cholesterol 593mg; Calcium 388mg; Fibre 3.8g; Sodium 636mg

Roast Duck with Orange and Drambuie

Sometimes classic combinations are the best, as is the case with duck and orange. Roast mallard accompanied by the bittersweet fruit has graced the dining tables of Europe for centuries in many guises; in this version the Scottish liqueur Drambuie is used to highlight the orange. This dish can be made in advance and reheated in the oven, sitting the duck pieces in the sauce. It is best accompanied with potatoes roasted in the duck fat and some peppery watercress.

Serves 4

2 mallards, plucked and cleaned
2 oranges, rind grated and reserved
2 thyme sprigs
2 bay leaves
5cm/2in cinnamon stick
75g/3oz/6 tbsp duck fat, softened
1 medium onion, finely chopped
2 garlic cloves, finely chopped
60ml/4 tbsp Drambuie
275ml/9fl oz/1 generous cup game or
    chicken stock
15ml/1 tbsp cornflour (cornstarch)
    mixed with an equal amount of water
sea salt and ground black pepper

1 Preheat the oven to 150°C/300°F/ Gas 2. Season the cavity of the duck with salt and pepper. Cut one orange in half and place half, with half the herbs and cinnamon stick, in each duck.

2 Rub the fat over the birds and season the skin before placing in a roasting pan and putting in the oven for 45 minutes. Baste the ducks occasionally with the fat from the pan.

3 After 45 minutes, baste once more, turn the oven up to 220°C/425°F/Gas 7 and cook for 10–15 minutes to crisp the skin. Remove the birds from the pan and leave to rest for 10 minutes.

4 Skim most of the fat from the cooking juices in the pan and set aside (see Cook's tip). Add the orange rind, chopped onion and garlic to the pan and cook, stirring, over medium heat for 5 minutes.

Cook's tip Any drained duck fat can be retained and stored in the refrigerator. It is perfect for roasting potatoes. However, with wild ducks there won't be nearly as much excess fat as with farm-reared birds.

5 Add the orange halves, cinnamon and herbs from the cooked ducks to the roasting pan, together with the juice of the second orange and the Drambuie.

6 As the Drambuie heats up, ignite the vapours with a match. Once the flames have died down add the stock, bring to the boil and simmer for 4 minutes.

7 Pour the cornflour mixture into the pan, stir and continue to simmer for 2 minutes as the sauce thickens. Strain and season to taste.

8 Remove the duck breasts from the bone and carve the legs from the carcass. Reheat in the sauce if necessary and serve with roast potatoes and watercress salad.

Energy 573kcal/2384kJ; Protein 34.7g; Carbohydrate 4.6g, of which sugars 0.9g; Fat 43g, of which saturates 15.7g; Cholesterol 235mg; Calcium 25mg; Fibre 0.2g; Sodium 191mg

Umbrian Roast Pheasant

In the rolling hills of Umbria in central Italy the cuisine is simple, reflecting the rural way of life. The region is famed for its rich, deep green olive oil, and its recipes, handed down from generation to generation, focus on quality ingredients and simple preparation. Serve with a spinach salad.

Serves 2

1 pheasant, drawn and cleaned
1 lemon, halved and thinly sliced
8 garlic cloves in their skins,
   lightly crushed
4 rosemary sprigs
75ml/2½fl oz/⅓ cup extra virgin
   olive oil
1 plump fennel bulb, cut into 10
   wedges through the root
12 baby potatoes, washed and halved
150ml/¼ pint/⅔ cup dry white wine
sea salt and ground black pepper
spinach salad, to serve

1 Preheat the oven to 200°C/400°F/ Gas 6. Place the pheasant in a bowl with the lemon, garlic and rosemary and season with salt and pepper. Rub the marinade into the flesh of the pheasant and leave for 30 minutes.

2 Meanwhile, heat the oil in a heavy roasting pan in the oven. Remove the pheasant from the marinade.

3 Place the bird on its side in the pan and roast in the oven for 15 minutes, then turn it on to its other side and roast for a further 15 minutes.

4 Remove the pan from the oven and turn the pheasant breast-side up. Place the fennel and potatoes around the bird, spooning the fat and juices over them, and return to the oven for 15 minutes.

5 Remove the roasting pan from the oven once more and add the lemon, garlic and rosemary sprigs, season and return to the oven for a final 15 minutes, by which stage the pheasant and vegetables should both be ready. Transfer the pheasant to a serving plate and keep warm.

6 Finally, add the wine to the roasting pan and bring to the boil over medium heat to combine the flavours of the vegetables and the cooking juices.

7 Carve the pheasant and serve with the vegetables and cooking juices, accompanied by spinach salad.

Energy 772kcal/3224kJ; Protein 67.2g; Carbohydrate 36.3g, of which sugars 6.5g; Fat 40.6g, of which saturates 10.1g; Cholesterol 460mg; Calcium 289mg; Fibre 7g; Sodium 327mg

Crispy Tarragon Pheasant

This pheasant is marinated for two days in a mixture of cream and mustard, which penetrates the meat so that it stays meltingly tender. Deep frying it means that the moist insides are complemented by the crispy fried skin of the pheasant, while the tangy, crunchy coleslaw makes a perfect accompaniment.

Serves 2

1 pheasant, drawn, cleaned
  and jointed
275ml/10fl oz/1⅛ cups double
  (heavy) cream
15ml/1 tbsp Dijon mustard
15ml/1 tbsp wholegrain mustard
15ml/1 tbsp chopped tarragon
2 sweet potatoes (400–450g/14–16oz)
15ml/1 tbsp vegetable oil
5ml/1 tsp black treacle (molasses)
sea salt and ground black pepper

For the coleslaw
275g/10oz white cabbage, shredded
1 carrot, grated
4 spring onions (scallions), chopped
1 small apple, grated
30ml/2 tbsp mayonnaise
5ml/1 tsp white wine vinegar
2.5ml/½ tsp caraway seeds

1 Put the pheasant in a bowl and add the cream, mustards, tarragon and lots of black pepper. Mix well, cover tightly and refrigerate for 48 hours, then remove the pheasant from the bowl and discard the marinade.

2 Preheat the oven to 200°C/400°F/ Gas 6. Place the sweet potatoes on a baking tray, rub with the vegetable oil, season and bake in the oven for about 45 minutes, depending on size. When the potatoes are soft all the way through, remove them from the oven and leave to cool slightly.

3 Meanwhile, make the coleslaw by mixing the cabbage, carrot, spring onions and apple with the mayonnaise, vinegar and caraway seeds. Season well with salt and pepper.

4 When the potatoes are cool enough to handle, cut them in half and scrape the flesh into a bowl. Add the treacle, salt and pepper and mix with a wooden spoon. Set aside and keep warm. Heat the deep fat fryer to 160°C/315°F.

5 When the oil is hot, place the pheasant pieces in the fryer basket and gently lower them into the oil. Fry for 8 minutes, then lift out the basket and increase the heat.

6 When the oil reaches 180°C/350°F lower the pheasant in again and fry for 4–5 minutes until golden and crispy. Remove and drain on kitchen paper. Season with salt and serve with the sweet potato purée and coleslaw.

Energy 1471kcal/6113kJ; Protein 66.4g; Carbohydrate 57.1g, of which sugars 29.1g; Fat 117.8g, of which saturates 52.2g; Cholesterol 650mg; Calcium 272mg; Fibre 9.1g; Sodium 791mg

Norfolk Pheasant Pasty

Cornwall claims that the pasty originated in south-west England, but this version hails from Norfolk in East Anglia. This region of England bursts with produce from both arable and livestock farming as well as game and orchard fruits, and this is a pasty that is packed with a little of everything. Served on its own as a tasty lunch, or accompanied by mashed potatoes and gravy for a hearty supper, it is the sort of food that keeps the farmers farming and the hunters hunting.

Makes 10

30ml/2 tbsp vegetable oil
1 small onion, finely diced
450g/1lb pheasant meat (boneless thigh or breast), minced (ground)
450g/1lb minced (ground) pork
115g/4oz smoked streaky (fatty) bacon very finely diced
pinch of ground cinnamon
pinch of ground ginger
5ml/1 tsp dried thyme
45ml/3 tbsp apple juice
50g/2oz/1 cup fresh white breadcrumbs
1 crisp eating apple (such as Cox), grated
30ml/2 tbsp parsley, chopped
15ml/1 tbsp sage, chopped
675g/1½lb/6 cups plain (all-purpose) flour, plus extra for rolling
350g/12oz lard, diced
2 eggs, beaten
sea salt and ground black pepper

1 Heat the oil in a large pan over medium heat. Place the onion, pheasant, pork, bacon, spices and thyme in the pan and cook, stirring occasionally, for 15 minutes.

2 Add the apple juice, breadcrumbs, apple, parsley and sage and season with plenty of salt and pepper. Stir to fully incorporate all the ingredients and cook for 5 minutes.

3 Reduce the heat to low and continue to cook for 10–15 minutes, stirring regularly to prevent the ingredients sticking to the pan. Transfer to a tray and leave to cool.

4 While the filling is cooling, make the pastry. Place the flour, lard and a generous pinch of salt in a bowl and rub the fat into the flour with your fingers, or cut it in with a knife. Add sufficient cold water (approximately 60ml/4 tbsp) to make a soft, pliable dough.

5 Form the dough into a ball, wrap in clear film (plastic wrap) and chill for at least 30 minutes. Preheat oven to 200°C/400°F/Gas 6.

6 Once the pastry has rested, dust the work surface with flour and roll out to a thickness of 3mm/⅛in.

7 Cut 10 circles out of the rolled pastry using a 15cm/6in bowl as a template. Re-roll the off-cuts if you need to.

8 Divide the filling evenly among the cases, spooning it into the centre; brush half the edge of each case with beaten egg and fold up over the filling.

9 Finish the pasties by crimping the edges between your thumb and fingers. Transfer to a baking sheet, well spaced and with the crimped edges uppermost.

10 Brush the pasties with the remaining egg and bake in the oven for 15 minutes, until golden. Allow to cool for 5 minutes before serving.

Cook's tip If short of time, use a 1kg/ 2¼lb pack of frozen puff or shortcrust pastry instead of making your own. Both the filling and the pastry can be made 2 days in advance and both freeze well, either separately or made into pasties.

Energy 751kcal/3137kJ; Protein 32.4g; Carbohydrate 57.8g, of which sugars 2.5g; Fat 42.2g, of which saturates 17.1g; Cholesterol 99mg; Calcium 134mg; Fibre 2.4g; Sodium 132mg

German-style Roast Goose

The goose is often eaten at Christmas throughout much of northern Europe and especially in Germany. A whole roast goose is often the centrepiece of the family feast on Christmas Eve. A wild goose, in comparison to its domesticated cousin, has had far more exercise and is subsequently much less fatty and can be a little tougher, calling for a slower roast and additional fat in which to cook the accompaniments. Wild goose is, however, much richer in flavour, and is well worth the extra care in cooking. This dish is served with roast potatoes and Brussels sprouts with bacon.

Serves 6

2 eating apples, cored and cut into
   12 slices each
12 pitted prunes
2 medium onions, chopped
2.5cm/1in cinnamon stick
1 thyme sprig
1 bay leaf
2.25kg/5lb goose, drawn and cleaned,
   reserving the neck, heart and liver
1.3kg/3lb potatoes such as King
   Edward, peeled and cut into
   4cm/1½in dice
115g/4oz/½ cup goose fat
50g/2oz/½ cup plain (all-purpose) flour
150ml/¼ pint/⅔ cup fruity German wine
about 600ml/1 pint/2½ cups game or
   chicken stock
sea salt and ground black pepper

For the Brussels sprouts with bacon

115g/4oz smoked streaky (fatty)
   bacon, diced
675g/1½lb Brussels sprouts, blanched
   in boiling water, cooled and halved
175g/6oz cooked chestnuts (vacuum
   packed or canned)
200ml/7floz/scant 1 cup white beer

1 Preheat oven to 160°C/325°F/Gas 3. Mix the sliced apples, prunes, half the onion, cinnamon stick, herbs, salt and pepper, then insert this stuffing into the cavity of the goose.

2 Prick the skin of the goose all over with a fork, season and place breast side down on a trivet in a roasting pan. Put the reserved goose neck in the bottom of the pan and add enough water to cover it. Roast for 1 hour, basting the goose every 20 minutes.

3 Turn the goose over, breast side up, and cook for a further hour, basting every 20 minutes, by which time the bird should be cooked. Remove from the oven, lift out the goose and set aside on a serving plate in a warm place to rest.

4 When the goose has been in the oven for 1¾ hours, put the potatoes into a pan of salted water, bring to the boil and cook rapidly for 8 minutes. Drain and allow the moisture to steam off for 2 minutes, return to the pan and shake to roughen the outsides. Keep warm.

5 Once the goose is cooked, increase the oven temperature to 220°C/425°F/Gas 7. Put 75g/3oz of the goose fat into a heavy baking tray and place in the oven to get very hot.

6 When the fat is spitting, carefully transfer the potatoes to the tray, turning them in the fat to coat them thoroughly. Season with salt and pepper and cook in the oven for 35–40 minutes, basting them every 10 minutes until they are golden and crisp.

7 Meanwhile, make the gravy. Remove the trivet from the roasting pan, add the heart, liver and remaining onion to the pan juices, and fry gently until softened.

8 Stir in the flour and cook for 3–4 minutes before adding the wine, the stock and approximately 600ml/1 pint/2½ cups water.

Energy 923kcal/3856kJ; Protein 50g; Carbohydrate 59.7g, of which sugars 19.7g; Fat 53.6g, of which saturates 8.1g; Cholesterol 18mg; Calcium 69mg; Fibre 5.6g; Sodium 258mg

9 Bring the gravy to a simmer, whisking as you do so and scraping the base of the pan to release any residue.

10 Pour the gravy into a pan and simmer gently for 30 minutes until smooth and glossy. Strain the gravy if you wish and keep warm.

11 While the gravy is simmering, prepare the Brussels sprouts. Place a frying pan over medium heat, add the remaining goose fat and the bacon pieces and cook gently for 5 minutes. Add the sprouts, turn up the heat and fry vigorously, turning, for 3 minutes. Add the chestnuts and beer and season. Bring to the boil and reduce the beer rapidly until the pan is nearly dry.

12 When everything is cooked, remove the sprouts and apple stuffing to a serving dishes, add the potatoes to the goose on the serving plate, and pour the gravy into a jug (pitcher). Carve the goose and serve.

Variation No German dinner table would be complete without some spiced, braised red cabbage.

Goose Hash with Fried Egg and Mustard Sauce

Wild goose is a seasonal treat, usually bagged in the autumn, when they are migrating south, which is why they are associated with Michaelmas and Christmas as roasts. As with many roasted big birds, the tastiest and most fulfilling of dishes are often those made from leftover scraps; there is something very satisfying about making a meal from next to nothing. For this recipe you will need the remains of a roast goose meal, including the meat picked from the bones, some cold roast potatoes and the fat collected from roasting. You can use the carcass to make stock for a further meal.

Serves 2

60ml/4 tbsp goose fat (or lard)
1 large onion, peeled, halved
  and sliced
2.5ml/½ tsp caster (superfine) sugar
450g/1lb cold roast potatoes, cut into
  1cm/½in dice
about 225g/8oz cold roast goose
  meat, chopped
15ml/1 tbsp chopped parsley
handful of greens or sprouting broccoli
2 goose eggs (or 4 duck or hen's eggs)
sea salt and ground black pepper

For the sauce

120ml/4fl oz/½ cup dry white wine
150ml/¼ pint/⅔ cup double
  (heavy) cream
10ml/2 tsp Dijon mustard

1 Heat a sizeable frying pan over medium heat and add 45ml/3 tbsp of the fat. Put the onion in the pan, season with the sugar, salt and pepper and fry, stirring occasionally, for about 12 minutes, until softened and golden.

Variation Any leftover game meat or a mixture of meats can be used in this recipe as a replacement for the goose. You could also try substituting the mustard with 10ml/2 tsp creamed horseradish.

2 Add the potatoes and goose, raise the heat and fry for a further 8 minutes, turning the ingredients in the pan from time to time to colour them all over.

3 Once everything is hot and coloured, stir in the parsley and keep warm.

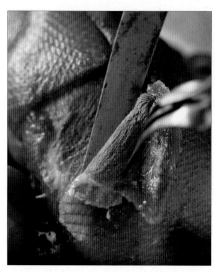

4 To make the sauce, pour the wine into a small pan and bring to the boil. Bubble for 15 seconds.

5 Add the cream to the wine and return to the boil for 15 seconds; stir in the mustard and turn off the heat. Season with salt and pepper and keep warm.

6 Blanch the greens in boiling water for 1 minute, then drain. Return to the pan, season with salt and pepper, cover and keep warm.

7 Transfer the hash to warmed plates and return the pan to the heat.

8 Heat the remaining fat in the pan and crack in the eggs. Cook until the white is set but the yolk is soft.

9 Serve the egg on top of the hash, with the greens on the side, covered in the creamy sauce.

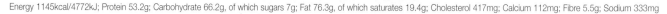

Energy 1145kcal/4772kJ; Protein 53.2g; Carbohydrate 66.2g, of which sugars 7g; Fat 76.3g, of which saturates 19.4g; Cholesterol 417mg; Calcium 112mg; Fibre 5.5g; Sodium 333mg

Rillette of Goose

Rillette, or potted meat, is a traditional preserve found throughout France. It is commonly made with goose or duck, but also with pork or rabbit or a mixture. For those with expensive tastes, the addition of foie gras can truly lift this peasant dish to another level. Using salted meat means that the rillette will last for weeks in the refrigerator if it is re-covered in fat each time it is used, making it a great standby. All it needs to go with it is some hot toast and some small gherkins or chutney.

Makes 1 jar

4 goose legs
1 thyme sprig
1 bay leaf
10 black peppercorns
4 juniper berries, lightly crushed
1 small onion, quartered
1 medium carrot, roughly sliced
1 celery stick, quartered
2 garlic cloves in their skins
50g/2oz/4 tbsp goose fat
15ml/1 tbsp chopped parsley
sea salt and ground black pepper

1 Place the goose legs in a bowl and add the herbs, peppercorns and juniper berries. Season liberally with salt, toss together and rub the salt into the flesh of the goose. Cover and refrigerate for 12–15 hours.

2 Preheat the oven 160°C/325°F/Gas 3. Rub the marinade off the goose legs, rinse them in cold water and pat dry. Discard the marinade ingredients.

3 Place the goose in a casserole with the vegetables and goose fat and just cover with water. Bring to a simmer.

4 Cover the dish and transfer to the oven for 3–4 hours, or until the flesh is falling off the bones. (Alternatively, cook on very low heat on the stove.) Check occasionally that there is enough liquid in the pan, topping it up if necessary.

5 Once the legs are completely cooked remove them to a tray to cool. Strain the stock from the pan, together with all the fat, to a bowl and leave to cool. Discard the vegetables.

6 Remove the skin from the goose and pull the meat off the bones, shredding it with your fingers as you do so. Lightly chop the meat and set it aside.

7 When the fat has solidified, separate it from the stock. Warm the fat and the stock in separate pans, so that the fat melts once more.

8 Place the shredded goose meat in a large bowl, add all but 30ml/2 tbsp of the melted fat and a little of the warmed stock and beat vigorously. Add a little more stock and beat again, taste for saltiness and continue to beat in as much stock as you can until the mixture is creamy and soft, and just salty enough without it being overbearing. Finally, beat in the chopped parsley.

9 Transfer to a jar or airtight container, smooth the top and pour over the reserved fat. Chill until needed. Serve with toast and gherkins or fruit chutney.

Energy 1727kcal/7161kJ; Protein 117.6g; Carbohydrate 0.4g, of which sugars 0.3g; Fat 139.3g, of which saturates 20.4g; Cholesterol 47mg; Calcium 70mg; Fibre 0.7g; Sodium 606mg

Southern Fried Turkey and Succotash

Wild turkey meat, soaked overnight in evaporated milk to tenderize it, makes a more than acceptable substitute for chicken in this recipe from the southern states of the USA. Southern fried chicken is famous the world over, and it is easy to see why: the crisply coated, lightly spiced and juicy meat is hard to turn down. To make this an all-American affair the turkey is partnered with succotash, a dish of white beans, corn and salad onions, which originated with the native North Americans.

Serves 4

1kg/2¼lb turkey breast and leg, boned
   and cut into thumb-sized strips
350ml/12fl oz can evaporated milk
2 eggs, beaten
175g/6oz/1½ cups plain
   (all-purpose) flour
10ml/2 tsp paprika
2.5ml/½ tsp cayenne pepper
2.5ml/½ tsp ground cinnamon
2.5ml/½ tsp ground ginger
pinch of turmeric
sea salt and ground black pepper

For the succotash
30ml/2 tbsp vegetable oil
1 large onion, diced
1 large carrot, finely diced
2 garlic cloves, chopped
2.5ml/½ tsp dried thyme
1 chicken stock (bouillon) cube
   dissolved in 200ml/7fl oz/scant
   1 cup hot water
400g/14oz can beans such as haricot
   (navy) or butter (lima), drained
250g/9oz can corn, drained
250ml/8fl oz/1 cup double
   (heavy) cream
12 spring onions (scallions),
   thinly sliced
sea salt and ground black pepper

1 Place the turkey, milk and egg in a bowl, mix well, cover and refrigerate for at least 12 hours, turning occasionally.

2 Next day, mix the flour, spices, two generous pinches of salt and lots of black pepper in a bowl.

3 Remove the turkey from the marinade and dredge in the seasoned flour to coat fully. Shake off any excess flour and lay on a wire rack to allow the flour to dry for 1–2 hours.

4 To make the succotash, heat a large pan over medium heat and add the oil. Add the onion, carrot, garlic and thyme and fry gently until completely soft, approximately 10 minutes.

Variation Grilled tomatoes and watercress go well with these two dishes, or you can eat southern fried turkey the traditional way, with fries, coleslaw and corn on the cob.

5 Add the stock to the vegetables and bring to the boil. Add the beans and corn, return to a simmer and cook gently for 4–5 minutes. Pour in the cream, bring back to a simmer for 2 minutes, then stir in the spring onions and season. Set aside and keep warm while you fry the turkey.

6 Preheat the deep fat fryer to 180°C/350°F. Arrange the pieces of turkey in the basket (you may need to do this in two batches, depending on the size of your fryer) and plunge them into the oil. Cook for approximately 10–12 minutes, shaking the basket from time to time to separate the pieces, until golden and crisp.

7 Drain the fried turkey on kitchen paper and season with salt to taste. Serve as soon as all the pieces are cooked, together with the succotash.

Energy 976kcal/4092kJ; Protein 75g; Carbohydrate 80.8g, of which sugars 20.8g; Fat 44.9g, of which saturates 20.9g; Cholesterol 207mg; Calcium 267mg; Fibre 10.5g; Sodium 723mg

Turkey Schnitzel, Spätzle and Pickled Mushrooms

If your wild turkey is too big for the oven, fillet out the breasts and use them in schnitzel – a thin, gently beaten escalope of meat with a crisp breadcrumb coating that is as Austrian as Vienna itself. The most famous variety must be the wiener schnitzel, which is made using veal, but the same method works with pork, chicken or in this case, turkey. Spätzle are a type of egg noodle, also much loved in Austria, where high carbohydrate foods help to combat the chill of the Alpine winter.

Serves 4

115g/4oz/1 cup seasoned flour
3 large eggs, beaten
250g/9oz/3 cups fine, dry breadcrumbs,
    mixed with 5ml/1 tsp finely chopped
    sage and 5ml/1 tsp finely chopped
    parsley, salt and pepper
675g/1½lb wild turkey breast, cut into
    4 slices and beaten out to a
    thickness of 3mm/¼in
30ml/2 tbsp vegetable oil
115g/4oz/½ cup butter
2 shallots, finely chopped
175g/6oz wild mushrooms such as
    ceps and chanterelles, sliced
grated rind and juice of ½ lemon
sea salt and ground black pepper

For the spätzle
300g/11oz/2¾ cups plain
    (all-purpose) flour
6 large (US extra large) eggs, beaten
nutmeg, salt and ground black pepper

1 Put the flour, beaten eggs and breadcrumbs in three separate trays or wide dishes. Season each flattened escalope with salt and pepper.

2 Turn the escalopes in the flour, then the beaten egg, shaking off any excess each time, and finally in the crumbs, patting gently to help the breadcrumbs adhere. Leave the coated escalopes to rest for at least 15 minutes before frying.

3 To make the spätzle dough, sift the flour into a bowl, add the beaten eggs, season with freshly grated nutmeg, salt and pepper and mix with a fork to make a smooth, pliable dough. Bring a large pan of salted water to the boil.

4 Scrape the dough on to a chopping board, divide roughly into two piles and, using the blade of a knife, push thin, noodle-shaped lengths of one half of the dough into the boiling water, dipping the blade of the knife into the water between each cut.

5 Simmer for 2 minutes, until the noodles float, then remove with a slotted spoon to a warm bowl, add 25g/1oz butter and toss to coat. Repeat with the second piece of dough. Keep the spätzle warm in a low oven.

Variation Breast of pheasant or guinea fowl would also work well, as would a steak cut from the leg of a wild boar.

6 Heat a large frying pan over medium to high heat and add the oil and half the butter in pieces. When it is foaming, arrange the turkey escalopes in the pan and fry for 3 minutes until golden on one side, then turn and cook for a further 3 minutes on the other side. Remove from the pan to a baking tray and keep warm in the oven.

7 Add the remaining butter to the pan over medium heat, add the shallot and fry until soft, then turn up the heat and add the mushrooms.

8 Cook vigorously, turning, until the mushrooms have softened. Season with salt and pepper, add the grated lemon rind and squeeze over the juice, allow to sizzle and remove from the heat.

9 To serve, arrange a pile of spätzle on each plate, topped with a turkey schnitzel and accompanied with a spoonful of mushrooms.

Energy 824kcal/3459kJ; Protein 55g; Carbohydrate 72.9g, of which sugars 3.6g; Fat 36.8g, of which saturates 18.1g; Cholesterol 292mg; Calcium 166mg; Fibre 3.1g; Sodium 820mg

VENISON, BOAR & GOAT

The various deer species offer the cook a wonderfully low-fat meat with hardly any wastage at all. There is a cut for every need: minced or ground meat from the shin and shoulder for the healthiest of burgers and cottage pies, large joints such as the shoulder or haunch for family gatherings, and the melt-in-the-mouth fillet and strip loin for that special dinner. Those who solely pursue boar and the various goat species have much in common with the hunters of deer – an organic, less contrived approach to shooting, where chance is celebrated. This chapter showcases these larger quarries, and their bounty, with recipes that make the most of the rich, flavoursome and adaptable cuts.

◄ *In Britain, herds of deer now face no danger from their natural predators, and culling is the only way to properly manage herd size and food availability.*

Roast Haunch of Roe Deer

When roasting venison it is important to add some fat. In this recipe, pork fat is pushed into the flesh, and the joint is marinated to ensure a moist finish. It is equally important not to overcook it.

Serves 6

1 roe deer haunch, weighing about
   2.5kg/5½lb
115g/4oz pork fat, cut into 10 strips
2 garlic cloves, cut into 10 strips
10 small rosemary sprigs
leaves from 2 thyme sprigs
60ml/4 tbsp olive oil
375ml/½ bottle ruby port
30ml/2 tbsp redcurrant jelly
sea salt and ground black pepper

For the potatoes
1.3kg/3lb potatoes such as Maris
   Piper, peeled and cut into chunks
175g/6oz/¾ cup beef dripping

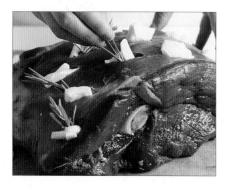

1 The evening before the meal, stab ten holes, evenly spaced, in the top surface of the meat, using the tip of a slender knife. Into each hole push a piece of pork fat, a sliver of garlic and a rosemary sprig.

2 Mix the thyme, 30ml/2 tbsp of the oil and the port. Place the joint in a wide dish and pour over the marinade. Leave it overnight in the refrigerator or a cool place, turning if possible.

3 The following day, preheat the oven to 220°C/425°F/Gas 7. Remove the venison from the marinade, reserving the liquid. Brush a roasting pan with the remaining oil, lay the meat in it and season with salt and pepper. Roast in the hot oven for 10 minutes.

4 Pour the marinade into the pan with the venison, reduce the temperature to 180°C/350°F/Gas 4 and cook for a further 30–40 minutes. Baste frequently.

5 Meanwhile, boil the potatoes in a large pan for around 5 minutes. Place a heavy roasting pan containing the dripping in the oven to heat. Drain the potatoes, return to the pan and shake vigorously; this will give them a crisper finish.

6 Set the roasting pan over low heat, place the potatoes in the fat, season with salt and pepper and turn to coat. Return the pan to the oven and cook for 40–50 minutes, turning once and basting after 30 minutes.

7 When the venison is cooked remove from the oven, strain the juices into a pan and leave to rest in a warm place.

8 Bring the pan of meat juices to a simmer and whisk in the redcurrant jelly. Serve the venison with the hot, crispy potatoes and redcurrant sauce.

Energy 1083kcal/4552kJ; Protein 65.6g; Carbohydrate 102.2g, of which sugars 15.3g; Fat 42.2g, of which saturates 15g; Cholesterol 152mg; Calcium 46mg; Fibre 6.1g; Sodium 184mg

Venison Heart Braised in Guinness

The heart is a wonderfully healthy meat, but having worked hard all its life it can be tough and is best cooked slowly. It produces a rich gravy, especially when cooked with stout, and to continue the Irish theme it is served with colcannon to soak up all the juices. The heart of a roe stag should be a good-sized portion for two; if using muntjak allow one heart per person.

Serves 2

115g/4oz minced (ground) pork
25g/1oz/½ cup soft white
   breadcrumbs
pinch of dried thyme
pinch of rubbed sage
grated rind of ½ lemon
3 gratings nutmeg
2 medium onions, diced
1 venison heart, washed and trimmed
50g/2oz/4 tbsp lard, dripping or butter
2 medium carrots, peeled and
   halved lengthways
1 celery stick, cut in 4 pieces
450ml/¾ pint/scant 2 cups Guinness
   or other stout
15ml/1 tbsp Worcestershire sauce
1 bay leaf
10ml/2 tsp cornflour (cornstarch)
sea salt and ground black pepper

For the colcannon
500g/1¼lb floury potatoes, peeled and
   cut into large dice
50g/2oz/¼ cup butter
15ml/1 tbsp chopped curly parsley
250g/9oz green cabbage, shredded
   and blanched for 2 minutes

1 Preheat the oven to 180°C/350°F/Gas 4. Put the pork, breadcrumbs, thyme, sage, lemon, nutmeg and half the onion in a bowl and mix well with your hands. Push the stuffing mixture into the heart cavities and season the outside with salt and pepper.

2 Heat the fat in an ovenproof pan and brown the heart on all sides. Remove from the pan and set aside.

3 Put the remaining onion, the carrot and celery in the pan and fry until beginning to soften. Return the heart to the pan with the Guinness, Worcestershire sauce and bay leaf.

4 Bring to a simmer, cover and put in the oven for 1¾–2 hours, or until the heart is tender.

5 Meanwhile, boil the potatoes in salted water until tender. Drain, return to the pan, add salt and pepper then mash with the butter and parsley. Stir in the blanched cabbage. Keep warm.

6 When the heart is done, remove the pan from the oven, mix the cornflour with a little water and whisk into the cooking juices. Return to the oven for 10 minutes to thicken the gravy.

7 Serve the heart carved crossways into four slices, with the vegetables, colcannon and gravy.

Energy 1042kcal/4348kJ; Protein 41.5g; Carbohydrate 84.5g, of which sugars 32.8g; Fat 56.3g, of which saturates 27.8g; Cholesterol 259mg; Calcium 204mg; Fibre 10.6g; Sodium 587mg

Seared Venison Carpaccio

Beef carpaccio was invented in the 1950s by Giuseppe Cipriani at Harry's Bar in Venice, Italy. In this version, venison fillet is briefly seared and given an extra black pepper kick; searing also eliminates any chance of contamination. The venison needs to be scrupulously trimmed. Carpaccio is usually served in paper-thin slices, but thicker slices mean you can really taste the quality of the meat.

Serves 4

400g/14oz trimmed venison fillet
60ml/4 tbsp extra virgin olive oil
20ml/4 tsp extra fine capers in brine
2 handfuls wild rocket (arugula)
12 shavings Parmesan cheese (about
   75–100g/3–3¾oz)
sea salt and ground black pepper
1 lemon, cut into wedges, to serve

3 When cool to the touch, remove the meat from the freezer and, using a very sharp knife, cut the fillet into thin slices across its length.

4 Drizzle with the remaining olive oil, sprinkle with salt and pepper, capers, rocket and Parmesan, and serve immediately with the lemon wedges.

1 Rub the meat with a little of the oil and rub in plenty of black pepper.

2 Heat a frying pan over high heat and seal the outside of the meat very rapidly, remove from the pan and place on a tray in the freezer to cool quickly.

Cook's tip If you prefer the meat to be sliced more finely, place the slices on a length of clear film (plastic wrap), sprinkle with a little water, cover with another length of film and roll gently with a rolling pin to achieve wafer-thin slices.

Energy 299kcal/1248kJ; Protein 31g; Carbohydrate 0.8g, of which sugars 0.8g; Fat 19.7g, of which saturates 6.2g; Cholesterol 69mg; Calcium 315mg; Fibre 1.1g; Sodium 330mg

Venison Agrodolce

The Italians frequently use an agrodolce or 'sweet and sour' element in game cooking, dating back to Roman times. The flavours are drawn from vinegar and fruit sugars, which blend to cut the richness of a meat such as venison. This dish can be cooked in advance: the flavours will mellow nicely over a couple of days. Be sure to allow at least a day to marinate before cooking. A typical Italian accompaniment for game dishes is pappardelle pasta, simply tossed in butter and fresh parsley.

Serves 6

1.5kg/3¼lb shoulder of venison,
    cut into 2.5cm/1in cubes
45ml/3 tbsp olive oil
100g/3¾oz pancetta, diced
1 medium onion, finely sliced
15ml/1 tbsp plain (all-purpose) flour
15ml/1 tbsp sultanas (golden raisins)
5ml/1 tsp ground cinnamon
5ml/1 tsp freshly grated nutmeg
30ml/2 tbsp pine kernels, toasted
50g/2oz 70% cocoa dark
    (bittersweet) chocolate
sea salt and ground black pepper
pappardelle pasta, to serve

For the marinade
400ml/14fl oz/1⅔ cups red wine
45ml/3 tbsp red wine vinegar
45ml/3 tbsp olive oil
1 medium carrot, thinly sliced
1 large onion, thinly sliced
1 celery stick, thinly sliced
3 garlic cloves, sliced
1 rosemary sprig
2 oregano sprigs
2 bay leaves
5ml/1 tsp juniper berries, crushed
ground black pepper

1 Mix all the marinade ingredients in a large bowl, add the meat and turn to coat thoroughly. Cover the bowl and leave to marinate in the refrigerator for 24–48 hours.

2 Remove the meat from the marinade, dry with kitchen paper and set aside. Strain the liquid and reserve, discarding the vegetables, herbs and spices.

3 Heat the oil in a heavy casserole and fry the pancetta gently until it is golden and the fat is rendered. Remove the pancetta from the pan and set aside. Preheat the oven to 150°C/300°F/Gas 2.

4 Season the meat with plenty of salt and pepper, turn the heat up and add the meat to the pan in batches to brown on all sides. When complete, set aside with the pancetta.

5 Reduce the heat, add the onions and fry until softened, sprinkle the flour over the onions and stir into the fat. Add the marinade liquid a little at a time, stirring constantly until it is all absorbed.

6 Bring to the boil, then return the pancetta and venison to the pan, together with the sultanas, spices and salt and pepper.

7 Return to the boil again, place a lid on the pan and cook in the hot oven for approximately 1½ hours. Check occasionally to make sure there is still some liquid in the pan, adding a little water if necessary.

8 Once the meat is tender, add the toasted pine nuts and, if serving immediately, stir in the chocolate. (If eating at a later date, add the chocolate just before serving.)

9 Serve the venison with freshly cooked pappardelle pasta, tossed in butter and chopped parsley.

Energy 528kcal/2216kJ; Protein 59.8g; Carbohydrate 10.3g, of which sugars 7.7g; Fat 24.5g, of which saturates 6.3g; Cholesterol 137mg; Calcium 30mg; Fibre 0.4g; Sodium 356mg

Venison Chilli con Carne

Chilli con carne is a staple of Tex-Mex cuisine. It is normally associated with beef but here venison is used instead. If you don't own a mincer or grinder, use finely diced meat, which gives a different – and some say better – texture. If you can, take half the meat from between the ribs, as this has some fat, and the rest from the shoulder or haunch. Serve the chilli with guacamole, tomato salsa, sour cream and tortilla chips to make a zingy supper dish that everyone will enjoy.

Serves 4

45ml/3 tbsp vegetable oil
1 large onion, diced
1 green (bell) pepper, diced
1 red (bell) pepper, diced
500g/1¼lb minced (ground) or
    diced venison
2 garlic cloves, sliced
2.5ml/½ tsp cayenne pepper
10ml/2 tsp smoked paprika
15ml/1 tbsp ground cumin
5ml/1 tsp ground coriander
400g/14oz canned chopped tomatoes
400g/14oz canned red kidney beans or
    black beans, drained and rinsed
15ml/1 tbsp tomato purée (paste)
sea salt and ground black pepper
tortilla chips, lime wedges and sour
    cream or crème fraîche, to serve

For guacamole and tomato salsa

1 large red onion, finely diced
2 mild or medium-hot red chillies,
    deseeded and finely diced
1 large very ripe avocado
4 large ripe tomatoes, chopped
2 limes
1 bunch fresh coriander (cilantro), half
    chopped, half reserved for garnish
sea salt

1 Heat a large, heavy pan over medium heat. Add the oil and fry the onions and peppers gently, stirring occasionally, until they soften.

2 Season the meat with salt and pepper and add to the pan, together with the garlic. Cook rapidly until the meat is browned then add the spices. Allow to cook for a further minute to release the oils from the spices.

3 Add the tomatoes, beans and 300ml/½ pint/1¼ cups water and bring to a simmer, stirring constantly.

4 Reduce the heat to low and cover the pan. If using minced (ground) meat, cook for 30–40 minutes until rich and thick. If using diced meat, cook for 1¼–1½ hours, stirring occasionally and adding water if necessary. Season to taste.

Cook's tip It's better to dice the meat finely or use a proper mincer than to chop it in a food processor, as the latter tends to produce too fine a texture.

5 To make the guacamole, place half the chopped onion in a bowl. Add one quarter of the chilli then scoop the avocado flesh into the bowl and crush with a fork to form a rough paste.

6 Put the rest of the chopped onion in a second bowl, with the remainder of the chopped chilli. Add the tomato flesh.

7 Grate the rind and squeeze the juice of one lime into each bowl and add a good pinch of salt to each. Mix each thoroughly and leave for 20 minutes to allow the flavours to mingle, before dividing the chopped coriander between the two bowls.

8 Divide the chilli con carne among four bowls and top with a tablespoon each of guacamole, tomato salsa and sour cream or crème fraîche. Garnish with coriander leaves and serve with a big bowl of tortilla chips and lime wedges on the side.

Energy 464kcal/1949kJ; Protein 39.1g; Carbohydrate 34.4g, of which sugars 16.5g; Fat 20.7g, of which saturates 4.2g; Cholesterol 63mg; Calcium 140mg; Fibre 11.6g; Sodium 487mg

Venison Steak with all the Trimmings

What could be better after a long day out hunting than a huge plate of steak and chips? It never fails to satisfy a big appetite, and with its high protein and high carbohydrate value it replaces all the energy used in the field. This recipe uses steaks from the rump, but loin or fillet would also be good.

Serves 2

vegetable oil for deep-frying
675g/1½lb Maris Piper potatoes, peeled and cut lengthways into 1cm/½in wide sticks
2 large ripe tomatoes, halved
2 large field mushrooms, cleaned
2 x 225–275g/8oz–10oz venison rump steaks, lightly pounded with a meat mallet or rolling pin
15ml/1 tbsp olive oil
1 bunch watercress
sea salt and ground black pepper

For the anchovy butter
115g/4oz/½ cup butter, softened
6 anchovy fillets, chopped
grated rind and juice of ½ lemon
2 garlic cloves, crushed
15ml/1 tbsp chopped parsley

1 First make the anchovy butter. Place the softened butter, anchovy fillets, lemon rind and juice, garlic and parsley in a bowl and whisk to blend. Beating or whisking it will make the butter light and fluffy – an electric hand whisk is best.

Cook's tip Double-frying the chips (French fries) means you can be sure that they are properly cooked on the inside and crisp on the outside; the perfect chips, in other words.

2 Transfer the anchovy butter to a length of clear film (plastic wrap) or baking parchment and roll into a cylindrical shape approximately 2.5cm/1in in diameter. Secure at the ends and refrigerate. This can be done in advance and the butter chilled or frozen.

3 Half an hour before eating, heat a deep fat fryer to 130°C/265°F. When the oil has reached this temperature, place the cut potatoes in the basket and blanch them for 8–10 minutes, until they are tender.

4 Remove the basket of chips (French fries) from the oil and raise the heat to 180°C/350°F. Preheat the grill (broiler).

5 Once the chips are blanched, place the tomato halves and mushrooms on a baking sheet and lay a thin slice of the flavoured butter on each. Season well with salt and black pepper, then place under a medium grill for 8–10 minutes, until cooked.

6 Meanwhile, heat a ridged griddle or frying pan over high heat. When it is hot, coat the steaks with olive oil and season well with salt and pepper,

7 Place the steaks on the hot griddle and cook for 2 minutes. Turn the steaks through 90 degrees and cook for 2 minutes more, turn over and repeat the process. You may want to increase the cooking time for a thick steak or if you prefer your meat well done.

8 When the steaks are cooked to your liking, remove them from the pan and set aside to rest.

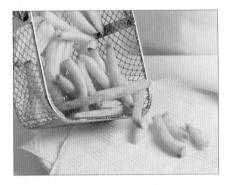

9 Refry the chips in the hot oil for 2 minutes, or until crisp on the outside and fluffy in the middle. Drain on kitchen paper and season with salt.

10 Slice the remaining butter, divide between the two steaks and place quickly under the grill, so it just starts to melt. Serve with chips, tomatoes and mushrooms, garnished with watercress.

Energy 1995kcal/8331kJ; Protein 70.4g; Carbohydrate 143.1g, of which sugars 5.8g; Fat 132.3g, of which saturates 47.3g; Cholesterol 245mg; Calcium 176mg; Fibre 11.9g; Sodium 1315mg

Daube of Venison

This classic French stew, with a hint of orange and lots of red wine, benefits from being allowed to sit overnight to improve the flavours. You can serve it as soon as it is cooked, if necessary, but it is better if you plan to make it a day ahead. Served with a creamy courgette gratin and some fresh crusty bread, it is the perfect dish to warm those late autumn evenings.

Serves 4

30ml/2 tbsp olive oil
1kg/2¼lb stewing venison (shin or
    chuck), cut into 2.5cm/1in cubes
150g/5oz unsmoked streaky (fatty)
    bacon, cut into lardons
12 shallots, peeled
15ml/1 tbsp plain (all-purpose) flour
375ml/½ bottle rich red wine, such
    as Burgundy
200ml/7fl oz/scant 1 cup venison
    stock or two beef stock (bouillon)
    cubes dissolved in 200ml/7floz/scant
    1 cup hot water
2 garlic cloves, crushed
2 bay leaves
1 thyme sprig
4 cloves
5cm/2in cinnamon stick
3 strips orange rind and juice of
    1 orange
200g/7oz Chantenay carrots, or 1 large
    carrot, sliced
2 celery sticks, sliced
25g/1oz dried wild mushrooms
    reconstituted in 50ml/2fl oz
    warm water
sea salt and ground black pepper
crusty bread, to serve

For the courgette gratin
25g/1oz butter
675g/1½lb courgettes (zucchini), diced
freshly grated nutmeg
250ml/8fl oz/1 cup double
    (heavy) cream
5ml/1 tsp thyme
1 garlic clove, crushed
75g/3oz Comté or Gruyère cheese
50g/2oz/1 cup fresh white
    breadcrumbs
10ml/2 tsp olive oil
sea salt and ground black pepper

1 Preheat the oven to 150°C/300°F/
Gas 2. Place a large casserole over high
heat and heat the oil.

2 Season the meat and fry until browned all over before adding the bacon. Cook for 2–3 minutes, then add the shallots and brown them too.

3 Sprinkle the flour over the meat and onions and stir in well. Add the wine and stock gradually, stirring to combine with the flour.

4 Add all the remaining ingredients to the pan, bring to a simmer, cover and transfer to the oven for 1½–1¾ hours. Remove from the oven when the meat is tender, correct the seasoning, cool and chill overnight.

5 About an hour before you want to serve, place the daube in a hot oven, preheated to 220°C/425°F/Gas 7.

Cook's tip If you have a slow cooker this is a perfect recipe for it. Long gentle simmering will only improve the flavours. However, it is still a good idea to cook it the day before you plan to eat it.

6 To make the gratin, butter a 30cm/
12in ovenproof dish and add the diced courgettes, nutmeg and seasoning.

7 Pour the cream over the courgettes and sprinkle over the thyme and garlic.

8 Mix the breadcrumbs and olive oil in a bowl, season, then spread over the gratin. Bake in the hot oven for 15–20 minutes, until the topping is crisp and the courgettes are tender.

9 When the daube is piping hot and the gratin is cooked, serve with fresh bread.

Energy 976kcal/4066kJ; Protein 72.1g; Carbohydrate 22.2g, of which sugars 9.4g; Fat 64.9g, of which saturates 31.7g; Cholesterol 261mg; Calcium 256mg; Fibre 3.4g; Sodium 924mg

Slow-roast Belly of Wild Boar

There are those who love fat and those that do not. This recipe can be enjoyed by both, as wild boar is much less fatty than its domestic cousins and this slow-cooked method renders the fat, basting the flesh as it cooks to leave a soft-textured meat with a lip-smacking stickiness. The crisp, bitter chicory complements the rich pork.

3 To make the salad dressing, put the mustard, maple syrup and vinegar in a bowl and whisk together. Gently drizzle in the light olive oil, whisking as you go to emulsify. Season well to taste, and set aside for the flavours to mingle.

4 When the meat has been cooking for 3 hours, halve the apples horizontally and remove the cores with a spoon.

5 In a heavy frying pan, gently heat the butter, sugar and thyme leaves, stirring. Place the apples cut side down in the mixture and cook gently for 5 minutes, moving them in the pan occasionally. Turn the apples, cover, and cook for 10–15 minutes until soft. Keep warm.

Serves 4

1.3kg/3lb wild boar belly, skin scored
15ml/1 tbsp olive oil
4 firm, tart green apples
50g/2oz/¼ cup butter
50g/2oz demerara (raw) sugar
1 thyme sprig, plus extra for garnish
3 heads chicory (Belgian endive), 2 white, 1 red, outer leaves and stems removed, leaves separated

For the salad dressing
10ml/2 tsp Dijon mustard
10ml/2 tsp maple syrup
5ml/1 tsp cider vinegar
30ml/2 tbsp light olive oil
sea salt and ground black pepper

1 Preheat the oven to 150°C/300°F/ Gas 2. Rub the pork all over with the olive oil and salt and pepper, rubbing it into the scores in the skin.

2 Place the pork, skin side up, in a sturdy roasting pan. Sprinkle with extra salt. Place in the oven for 3½–4 hours.

6 When the belly is cooked, remove from the oven and leave to rest for 10 minutes. Carve into eight slices, two for each serving. Arrange the meat on warm plates with two halves of apple each and some chicory leaves. Drizzle the chicory with the maple and mustard dressing and garnish with thyme.

Energy 1499kcal/6203kJ; Protein 50.6g; Carbohydrate 24.1g, of which sugars 22.4g; Fat 134.6g, of which saturates 50.7g; Cholesterol 263mg; Calcium 56mg; Fibre 1.9g; Sodium 415mg

Wild Boar, Chickpea, Saffron and Pepper Stew

Even in summertime, a well-cooked stew is always a welcome sight. This recipe is light, sweet with olive oil and full of summer colours created by the saffron, red peppers and deep green of the parsley. The dish is well complemented by a crunchy mixed salad and a big dollop of fiery rouille.

Serves 4

175ml/6fl oz/¾ cup virgin olive oil
1 large onion, roughly chopped
1 celery stick, roughly chopped
225g/8oz carrots, diced
4 garlic cloves, peeled and halved
2.5ml/½ tsp dried chilli flakes
7.5ml/1½ tsp fennel seeds
7.5ml/1½ tsp cumin seeds
5ml/1 tsp dried thyme or oregano
2 bay leaves
675g/1½lb shoulder of boar, cubed
1 large red (bell) pepper, chopped
good pinch of saffron strands
275ml/9fl oz/1 generous cup dry
    white wine
400g/14oz can chopped tomatoes
2 x 400g/14oz cans chickpeas,
    drained and rinsed
flat leaf parsley, roughly chopped

For the rouille
6–8 saffron strands
1 slice stale white bread, crust
    removed, torn into pieces
2 garlic cloves, crushed to a paste
5ml/1 tsp harissa paste (or more)
2 egg yolks
10ml/2 tsp lemon juice
425ml/15fl oz/1¾ cups light olive oil
sea salt and ground black pepper

1 Heat a large pan, add the oil, onion, celery and carrot and cook, stirring occasionally, until softened. Add the garlic, spices and herbs and cook for a further 2 minutes, still stirring,

2 Add the boar meat and red pepper, and cook until the meat has changed colour. Add the saffron and wine and bring to the boil to drive off the acidity.

3 Add the tomatoes and chickpeas. Bring to a simmer, loosely cover with a lid and reduce the heat to very low.

4 Cook gently for 1½–1¾ hours, stirring occasionally, until the meat is tender, then add the parsley.

5 To make the rouille, put the saffron strands in a bowl, pour over 30ml/2 tbsp boiling water and allow to steep (infuse) for 5 minutes. Add the torn bread, crushed garlic and harissa paste, stir together and leave to stand so that the liquid soaks into the bread. Use a fork to crush the ingredients to a paste.

6 Put the egg yolks into a bowl with the lemon juice and whisk to combine. Slowly drizzle the oil on to the mixture, whisking continuously. Once all the oil is incorporated, add the soaked bread mixture and season to taste.

7 Serve the stew in four warmed bowls, and top each one with a big spoonful of the rouille.

Energy 803kcal/3351kJ; Protein 50.9g; Carbohydrate 43g, of which sugars 13.9g; Fat 43.8g, of which saturates 7.5g; Cholesterol 106mg; Calcium 133mg; Fibre 11g; Sodium 537mg

Sticky Wild Boar Ribs with Boston Baked Beans

These two great American classics work really well with wild boar, the cola-braised ribs and slow-baked beans combining to make a deeply satisfying supper dish. The recipe calls for baby back ribs, which are those to which the loin is attached. If butchering them yourself, don't cut too close up the rib to leave a little more flesh. The beans are known in the USA as navy beans, because they were a staple on board ship. Dried beans require soaking overnight, so begin the day before.

Serves 6

For the Boston baked beans
450g/1lb/2½ cups haricot (navy) beans,
    soaked in cold water overnight
1 large onion, finely chopped
30ml/2 tbsp Dijon mustard
40g/1½oz/3 tbsp soft dark brown sugar
40g/1½oz/3 tbsp soft light brown sugar
75g/3oz/¼ cup treacle (molasses)
225g/8oz belly pork, cut into chunks
2 bay leaves
15ml/1 tbsp ground black pepper
sea salt

For the sticky wild boar ribs
250ml/8fl oz/1 cup cola
60ml/4 tbsp cider vinegar
250g/9oz/1 generous cup soft
    dark brown sugar
2 red chillies, deseeded and chopped
2 racks baby back ribs (about
    2kg/4½lb)
sea salt and ground black pepper

3 Add the onion, mustard, sugars, treacle, belly pork, bay leaves and black pepper to the beans and stir well.

4 Add sufficient reserved bean liquor to just cover the beans, cover and place in the oven for 2½–3 hours. Check every 30 minutes to ensure the beans are not drying out, adding more of the cooking liquor if necessary.

5 Meanwhile, put the cola, vinegar, sugar and chillies for the sticky ribs into a pan and gently heat, stirring, until the sugar has dissolved. Turn the heat up and reduce the liquid to a sticky syrup. Set aside.

Cook's tip The Boston baked beans will keep well for a day or two, and their flavour will improve. They can also be frozen, so you could make double quantities, freeze half and defrost when you next have a rack of ribs to roast.

6 When the beans have been in the oven for 1½ hours it is time to start the ribs. Season them well with salt and pepper and rub it into the flesh. Place the ribs into a large roasting pan, cutting them into shorter pieces if necessary.

7 Cover the roasting pan with foil and put into the oven along with the beans for 1½ hours, until the meat is tender and the beans are cooked. Remove both from the oven and increase the temperature to 220°C/425°F/Gas 7. Season the beans with salt to taste.

8 Coat the ribs with the cola syrup and return to the oven uncovered. Cook for 10 minutes, then turn, baste and cook for a further 5–10 minutes.

9 The cola should be almost completely reduced at this point; baste the ribs with any remaining syrup and leave to rest for 5 minutes before carving and serving with the beans.

1 Drain the beans, place in a large casserole and cover with fresh water, bring rapidly to the boil and drain again. Return the beans to the pan, cover with water, bring to the boil and skim. Simmer gently for 45–60 minutes, or until the skins just begin to break.

2 Preheat the oven to 160°C/325°F/Gas 3. Drain the beans, reserving the cooking liquor, and return to the pan.

Energy 818kcal/3431kJ; Protein 53g; Carbohydrate 75.5g, of which sugars 43.5g; Fat 35.8g, of which saturates 13.4g; Cholesterol 130mg; Calcium 188mg; Fibre 12.3g; Sodium 209mg

Wild Boar Hock with Buckwheat Dumplings

This recipe originates from the Czech Republic but it is in a style typical of dishes found in parts of Eastern Europe where wild boar is still hunted. Several hours of cooking result in melt-in-the-mouth tenderness and a deliciously sticky sauce. The dumplings are made predominantly with potato, but the addition of some buckwheat flour lightens them and adds a sweet, nutty flavour.

Serves 2

1 wild boar hock
1 large onion, finely chopped
4 garlic cloves, peeled
115g/4oz smoked streaky (fatty)
    bacon, cut in 2 pieces
30ml/2 tbsp paprika
1 litre/1¾ pints/4 cups apple juice
3 medium turnips, peeled and
    halved (reserving the green tops
    if available)
12 sage leaves
sea salt and ground black pepper

For the dumplings
500g/1¼lb floury potatoes in their
    skins, scrubbed
115g/4oz/1 cup buckwheat flour
50g/2oz/½ cup plain (all-purpose) flour
1 small (US medium) egg, beaten
50g/2oz/¼ cup butter
the reserved turnip tops or a
    good handful of baby spinach,
    finely shredded
sea salt and ground black pepper

1 Place the hock in a large pan with the onion, garlic, bacon, paprika and apple juice. Season and mix well. Bring gently to the boil, removing any scum.

2 Turn the heat down to very low, cover with a tight-fitting lid and cook gently for 3 hours, checking the level of the cooking liquid occasionally.

3 Once the meat is starting to leave the bone, add the turnips and sage to the pan and cook, uncovered, for a further 15 minutes. If the cooking juices are a little thin, decant them into a second pan and reduce.

4 Gently boil or steam the potatoes in their skins for 15–20 minutes until tender. Drain and allow any moisture to evaporate from the skins.

5 Meanwhile, bring a second pan of salted water to the boil.

6 Peel the potatoes while still hot (either hold them in a cloth or wear rubber gloves). Place the potatoes in a large bowl and mash thoroughly, or put them through a ricer.

7 Add the buckwheat and plain flours to the mashed potato and mix well, you may find it easiest to do this with your hands. Then add the beaten egg and mix again to a smooth dough-like paste.

8 Roll the dough into a sausage shape and cut into 2.5cm/1in lengths. When the pan of water has come to the boil drop the dumplings into the water and cook for about 1 minute until they rise to the surface, then remove to a tray.

9 To finish the dumplings, warm a frying pan and add the butter. When it begins to foam, add the dumplings and fry until just colouring.

10 Add the shredded greens to the dumpling pan, together with plenty of salt and pepper, and toss until wilted.

11 Serve the hock casserole together with the dumplings and greens on warmed plates.

Variation If you want a really rich side dish, arrange the dumplings in a gratin dish, spoon over plenty of sour cream and brown under a hot grill (broiler).

Energy 1291kcal/5442kJ; Protein 59.8g; Carbohydrate 171.5g, of which sugars 65.3g; Fat 45.8g, of which saturates 21.5g; Cholesterol 285mg; Calcium 290mg; Fibre 9.6g; Sodium 1114mg

Crofter's Pie

Crofting has been a way of life for many years in Scotland; these agricultural smallholdings in the far reaches of the highlands and islands rely mainly on sheep farming, often supplemented with wild fish and game. Feral goats, ancestors of escaped domestic animals, roam wild in some parts of Scotland, and when the weather is moving in from the North Atlantic it's time to stay inside, light the fire and dish up a comforting winter warmer topped with Scotland's traditional neeps 'n' tatties.

Serves 6

1 shoulder of goat on the bone, cut
    through the knee joint
3 medium carrots, peeled and diced
1 large onion, peeled and diced
2 celery sticks, diced
1 large leek, diced, washed
    and drained
15ml/1 tbsp tomato purée (paste)
2 rosemary sprigs
2 bay leaves
115g/4oz/½ cup butter
50g/2oz/½ cup plain (all-purpose) flour

For the neeps 'n' tatties

900g/2lb swede (rutabaga), peeled and
    cut into small chunks
900g/2lb potatoes, peeled and cut into
    large chunks
6 gratings of nutmeg
sea salt and ground black pepper

1 Preheat the oven to 180°C/350°F/ Gas 4. Place the meat, carrots, onion, celery, leek, tomato purée and herbs in a large casserole with 1 litre/1¾ pints/4 cups water and plenty of salt and pepper. Bring to a simmer, cover and place in the oven for 2 hours.

Cook's tip This dish can be made in advance and reheated. Keep the oven temperature to 150°C/300°F/Gas 2 until the centre of the pie is piping hot and then increase the heat to brown the top.

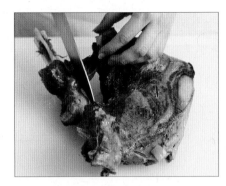

2 After 2 hours the meat should be tender and falling off the bones. Remove the joint from the pan and strip off the meat, discarding the bones. Chop the meat into small chunks. Strain the stock, reserving it and the vegetables.

3 In a second pan melt half the butter, add the flour and stir to form a thick paste. Cook for 2 minutes, stirring constantly, until the roux is pale in colour and has a grainy consistency. Gradually add the stock, stirring and allowing the gravy to thicken between each ladleful.

4 Once all the stock has been incorporated, return it to the original pan with the vegetables and chopped meat. Check for seasoning at this point. Stir everything together and cook over low heat for 15–20 minutes, until the gravy is thick and rich. Turn the oven temperature up to 220°C/425°F/Gas 7.

5 While the gravy is thickening, prepare the neeps 'n' tatties. Put the swede in a pan of salted water and bring to the boil, then lower the heat and simmer for 2 minutes. Add the potatoes, return to the boil and simmer for 12 minutes or until soft but not breaking up.

6 Drain the swede and potatoes in a colander and leave for 2 minutes to allow any moisture to steam off. Melt the remaining butter in the pan with the nutmeg, then return the swede and potatoes to the pan, season with salt and pepper and mash roughly.

7 Top the cooked goat with the neeps 'n' tatties and return the dish to the oven for 20 minutes to brown the topping before serving.

Variation If you want to make the pie richer, and give it an even more Scottish flavour, add some cooked haggis to the meat in step 4.

Energy 957kcal/3982kJ; Protein 52.3g; Carbohydrate 41.8g, of which sugars 15.7g; Fat 65.7g, of which saturates 33.3g; Cholesterol 247mg; Calcium 142mg; Fibre 6.9g; Sodium 364mg

Braised Shoulder of Goat with Anchovy

This is one of those one-pot dishes in which all the flavours of the ingredients blend to make a deeply satisfying meal. Salted anchovies have been enriching meat dishes for hundreds of years, since at least the time of the ancient Romans, and here they enhance the goat meat perfectly.

Serves 6

10 salted anchovies, chopped
8 garlic cloves, chopped
rind and juice of 1 lemon
2 sprigs rosemary, picked
   and chopped
30ml/2 tbsp olive oil
1 shoulder of goat, boned (reserving
   the bone to flavour the gravy)
3 medium carrots, peeled and diced
2 medium onions, peeled and diced
2 celery sticks, diced
2 bay leaves
2 thyme sprigs
300ml/½ pint/1¼ cups red wine
115g/4oz/½ cup Puy lentils
6 small turnips, peeled and halved
ground black pepper

1 Combine the anchovies, garlic, lemon rind and rosemary. Lay the joint skin-side down and rub the anchovy mixture into the meat. Season with pepper and roll back into a shoulder shape, using string to tie the meat quite tightly at intervals. Season the outside. Preheat the oven to 180°C/350°F/Gas 4.

2 Heat the oil in a large casserole. Place the meat in and colour on all sides. Lift out the meat and set aside; add the carrots, onions and celery to the pan.

3 When the vegetables are soft, add the bay leaves, thyme and red wine. Simmer for 2 minutes. Return the meat to the pan with the bone and 500ml/17fl oz/ generous 2 cups water. Bring to the boil, cover and place in the oven for 1¼ hours.

4 Remove the pan from the oven and stir in the lentils. Bring back to the boil, cover and return to the oven.

5 After 30 minutes the meat should be soft to the touch and the lentils tender. Add the turnips and return to the oven for a further 10 minutes.

6 Lift out the meat and leave to rest for 10 minutes. Remove the string and carve into six thick slices. Divide the meat and vegetables between six bowls and squeeze the lemon juice over each.

Energy 1106kcal/4585kJ; Protein 54.2g; Carbohydrate 18.5g, of which sugars 8.3g; Fat 87.4g, of which saturates 27.9g; Cholesterol 203mg; Calcium 98mg; Fibre 4.7g; Sodium 398mg

Chunky Goat Moussaka

Versions of moussaka are found from Syria to Greece, and though it's usually made from lamb or mutton, goat is often substituted. Instead of the thick white sauce topping commonly added in Western Europe, this recipe uses thick natural yoghurt, which gives a welcome tang to a rich dish.

Serves 6

90ml/6 tbsp olive oil
1.3kg/3lb shoulder of goat, diced
1 large onion, finely chopped
1 large carrot, finely chopped
1 celery stick, finely chopped
6 garlic cloves, finely diced
5ml/1 tsp cumin seeds
5ml/1 tsp fennel seeds
pinch of dried red chilli flakes
5cm/2in cinnamon stick
5ml/1 tsp dried thyme
5ml/1 tsp dried oregano
2 bay leaves
10ml/2 tsp paprika, plus extra
  for sprinkling
2 x 400ml/14oz cans tomatoes
375ml/½ bottle dry white wine
3 medium aubergines (eggplants),
  sliced 1cm/½in thick, sprinkled with
  salt and left to drain for 30 minutes
900ml/1½ pints/3¾ cups thick
  natural (plain) yogurt
salt and ground black pepper
tomato salsa, to serve (see Cook's tip)

1 Heat a large pan and add 60ml/4 tbsp of the olive oil. Season the meat and brown, stirring from time to time.

Cook's tip To make the tomato salsa, chop 9 ripe tomatoes, thinly slice 1 red onion, chop a handful of flat leaf parsley and place in a bowl with 24 pitted black olives, 45ml/3 tbsp white wine vinegar, 30ml/2 tbsp extra virgin olive oil, salt and pepper. Toss together and serve.

2 Add the vegetables, cumin, fennel, chilli and cinnamon and continue to fry until soft. Stir in the herbs, paprika, tomatoes and wine, season with salt and pepper and bring to a simmer. Cover and cook gently for 1½ hours, stirring occasionally, until the meat is tender and the sauce thick and rich.

3 Heat a large frying pan, pat the aubergines dry, season with pepper and fry in the remaining oil until golden.

4 Preheat the oven to 200°C/400°F/ Gas 6, then assemble the moussaka.

5 Cover the base of a 30x20cm/12x8in baking dish with half the meat sauce; cover this with a layer of half the aubergine then repeat the layers. Spread the yogurt over the top, and sprinkle with a little paprika. Bake in the preheated oven for 20–30 minutes until heated through and golden on top. Serve with tomato salsa.

Energy 693kcal/2883kJ; Protein 40.7g; Carbohydrate 23.3g, of which sugars 22.1g; Fat 45.1g, of which saturates 17.3g; Cholesterol 134mg; Calcium 340mg; Fibre 4.7g; Sodium 262mg

Casserole of Goat with Lettuce and Peas

With the onset of summer comes the pleasure of market stalls bulging with new seasonal produce. This light casserole is full of those early summer foods: new potatoes, peas, lettuce, baby onions and mint give a sweet finish to the gravy. Cooking salad leaves may seem a little odd but lettuce and peas have long been combined in French cuisine; the leaves have a delicate flavour and silky texture.

Serves 6

30ml/2 tbsp olive oil
1 large leg of goat, boned, trimmed of
  sinew and cut into 2.5cm/1in cubes
  (reserve the bone for stock)
115g/4oz/1 cup seasoned plain
  (all-purpose) flour
175g/6oz/¾ cup butter
1 large carrot, cut into 4 pieces
1 celery stick, cut into 4 pieces
1 medium onion, cut into 4 wedges
  through the root
15cm/6in length of white of leek
6 garlic cloves
10ml/2 tsp tomato purée (paste)
375ml/½ bottle dry white wine
2 bay leaves
1 thyme sprig
12 shallots
30 small new potatoes, scrubbed
  and boiled
3 plump Little Gem (Bibb) lettuces, cut
  into quarters through the root
450g/1lb/4 cups shelled peas,
  blanched in unsalted water (frozen
  are a good substitute)
good handful of fresh mint
  leaves, chopped
sea salt and ground black pepper

1 Warm a large casserole, add the oil and turn the heat up. Dust the pieces of goat in the seasoned flour, shaking off any excess.

2 Fry the meat in batches until browned on all sides, removing and reserving the pieces as they are done. When all the meat is browned, reduce the heat a little and add 50g/2oz/¼ cup of the butter. Cook the carrot, celery and onion until coloured, then add the leek and garlic.

3 When the vegetables are soft, stir in the tomato purée. Add the white wine and herbs and bring to a simmer. Preheat the oven to 180°C/350°F/Gas 4.

Cook's tip To make stock, roast about 3kg/6lb bones with 1 carrot, 1 onion and 1 celery stick, cut into chunks, in a hot oven until the bones are browned, then remove to a stock pot. Add 15ml/ 1 tbsp tomato purée (paste), 1 bay leaf and 1 thyme sprig, cover with water and bring to the boil. Skim off any fat and scum, reduce the heat and simmer for 4 hours. Strain the stock and boil rapidly to reduce to about 900ml/1½ pints/ 3¾ cups. This can be made up to 4 days in advance or frozen for future use.

4 Simmer the wine for 2 minutes before returning the goat to the pan along with the reserved bone and 900ml/1½ pints/3¾ cups water, or preferably stock (see Cook's tip). Bring the contents of the pan to the boil, skim off any scum, cover the pan and place in the oven for 1¼–1½ hours, or until the goat is tender.

5 Remove the meat from the pan, strain the sauce and discard the vegetables and the bone. Return the meat and sauce to the pan.

6 In a large frying pan, melt 50g/2oz/ ¼ cup of the remaining butter and gently sauté the shallots until golden. Add the onions and cooked potatoes to the meat, stir into the sauce and heat gently for 2 minutes to warm through.

7 Add the lettuce to the pan and cook for a further 2 minutes before stirring in the peas and the remaining butter. Just before serving, add the mint.

Energy 1005kcal/4177kJ; Protein 59.1g; Carbohydrate 35.2g, of which sugars 11.1g; Fat 66.4g, of which saturates 28.9g; Cholesterol 260mg; Calcium 112mg; Fibre 6.7g; Sodium 381mg

RABBIT, HARE & SQUIRREL

The rough shooter is unencumbered by etiquette requirements, any kind of dress code and the inevitable tips of fellow guns. With fewer expectations and considerably less financial outlay, the only concerns are personal safety, nature's own slideshow and what the spoils will be. The shooter will delight at whatever a hedgerow or a field of sugar beet may conjure up. Similarly, the silent pigeon shooter, hardly moving, squinting up as the first few pigeons of dusk come floating into the treetops, won't fail to grab the opportunity of a squirrel scuttling towards a drey or the first rabbits appearing for their evening graze. These creatures, regarded as pests for the havoc they wreak on farm and woodland, will make some of the tastiest dishes you could possibly wish for.

◄ *The snap of a twig underfoot and suddenly your quarry – and lunch if your shot is true – is startled into your sights.*

Potted Rabbit

If you have several rabbits, preserve some of the meat using this traditional, thrifty recipe. Potted meat has been made for centuries in rural communities all over Europe, and it keeps for weeks in the refrigerator. To serve, it needs nothing more with it than some hot toast and pickles.

**Fills a 1-litre/1¾-pint/4-cup
storage jar**

2 rabbits, cleaned and gutted,
   sprinkled with 50g/2oz/¼ cup sea
   salt and refrigerated overnight
115g/4oz pork shoulder, diced
800g/1¾lb/3½ cups duck or goose fat
4 cloves
12 peppercorns
2.5cm/1in cinnamon stick
2 blades mace or 8 gratings nutmeg
4 garlic cloves, unpeeled
2 thyme sprigs
1 bay leaf
1 large carrot, very finely diced
1 medium leek, finely diced
sea salt and ground black pepper
hot toast and gherkins, to serve

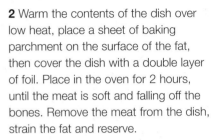

1 Rinse the rabbits in cold water, dry and cut into joints. Place the rabbit and pork in a heatproof dish big enough to hold all the meat in one layer. Melt the duck or goose fat and pour it over the meat, then add the spices, garlic and herbs. Preheat the oven to 140°C/275°F/Gas 1.

2 Warm the contents of the dish over low heat, place a sheet of baking parchment on the surface of the fat, then cover the dish with a double layer of foil. Place in the oven for 2 hours, until the meat is soft and falling off the bones. Remove the meat from the dish, strain the fat and reserve.

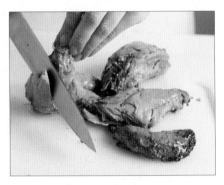

3 While the meat is still warm, strip it from the bones and chop finely, checking for bone fragments. Place in a large bowl and keep warm.

4 Gently fry the carrot until soft, in a little of the fat, add the leek and cook until soft. Mix into the meat with a ladleful of fat. Beat to incorporate. Add another ladleful of fat and beat again, and repeat until the mixture will hold no more fat – about 3–4 ladlefuls. Season to taste.

5 Sterilize the jar, and while still hot fill with the rabbit mixture. If there is still room in the jar top it up with more fat, seal. When cool store in the refrigerator. Serve piled on to toast, with gherkins.

Energy 8502kcal/35083kJ; Protein 243.6g; Carbohydrate 13.7g, of which sugars 11.8g; Fat 830.4g, of which saturates 345.3g; Cholesterol 1651mg; Calcium 479mg; Fibre 6.8g; Sodium 622mg

Polish Hunter's Stew

Hunter's stew, or bigos, is a popular dish in Poland and there are many variations. The name translates as 'hotchpotch', and it can be made with whatever game you have bagged or bought. A big hearty stew like this deserves a big hearty accompaniment, so serve with mashed potato.

Serves 8

75g/3oz/6 tbsp lard or duck fat
1 good-sized rabbit, jointed, saddle
    cut into 4
2 pheasant legs, cut into 4 pieces,
4 pigeons, breasts and legs removed,
250g/9oz smoked dry-cured streaky
    (fatty) bacon, cut into 1cm/½in dice
2 onions, chopped
2 carrots, diced
500g/1¼lb jar sauerkraut, drained
500g/1¼lb white cabbage, shredded
40g/1½oz dried porcini soaked in
    600ml/1 pint/2½ cups hot water
250ml/8fl oz/1 cup red wine
4 tomatoes, skinned and chopped
15ml/1 tbsp honey
2 bay leaves
30ml/2 tbsp fresh or dried marjoram
10ml/2 tsp caraway seeds
5ml/1 tsp juniper berries, crushed
900ml/1½ pints/3¾ cups good stock
250g/9oz sausages such as Wieska
    (Polish village sausage)
10 prunes, pitted and chopped
sea salt and ground black pepper

1 Heat the fat in a large casserole. Season the pieces of game and fry in batches, browning on all sides and then setting aside.

2 Add the bacon to the pan and cook gently to render the fat. Add the onions and carrots to the pan and cook, stirring occasionally, until soft.

3 Add the sauerkraut and shredded cabbage, and continue to fry gently.

4 Add the sausage and prunes to the pan and season to taste. Cover and continue to cook for 45 minutes until the meat begins to fall off the bone.

5 Return the meat to the pan, add the mushrooms and their soaking liquor, the wine, tomatoes, honey, herbs, caraway seeds, juniper berries and stock. Bring to a simmer, cover and cook gently for 45 minutes, stirring occasionally. Add a little extra wine or water during cooking if the pan is becoming dry.

Energy 499kcal/2076kJ; Protein 33g; Carbohydrate 15.2g, of which sugars 11.9g; Fat 31g, of which saturates 11.9g; Cholesterol 96mg; Calcium 132mg; Fibre 4.7g; Sodium 1079mg

English Rabbit and Game Pie

A quintessential element of the English buffet table has to be a hot water pastry pie. Whether it is pork, game or veal and ham, the lard-rich pastry encasing it is always a welcome sight. The main meat ingredient in this recipe is rabbit, but it could be a mix of any game; a little fatty pork is always needed, though. Make sure you leave enough time to make the jelly, as this needs to cook for 6 hours.

Serves 10–12

For the pie filling
1kg/2¼lb rabbit flesh, diced
300g/11oz partridge flesh, diced
300g/11oz pigeon flesh, diced
300g/11oz fatty pork belly,
   minced (ground) or chopped in
   a food processor
grated rind of 1 lemon
15ml/1 tbsp chopped sage
15ml/1 tbsp chopped thyme
2.5ml/½ tsp freshly grated nutmeg
15ml/1 tbsp English (hot)
   mustard powder
60ml/4 tbsp ruby port
sea salt and ground black pepper

For the jellied stock
2 pig's trotters (feet), split lengthways
   rabbit and game bones
1 carrot, peeled
1 small onion, peeled
1 bay leaf

For the pastry
150g/5oz/⅔ cup lard
150g/5oz/⅔ cup butter
350ml/12fl oz/1½ cups water
850g/1lb 14oz/7½ cups plain
   (all-purpose) flour
good pinch of sea salt
1 egg, beaten, to glaze

1 The jelly must be made in advance. Place the ingredients in a pan, cover with plenty of water, bring to the boil and skim off any scum and fat. Reduce the heat to a simmer and cook for 6 hours, skimming and topping up with water as necessary.

2 At the end of the cooking time, strain the liquid and discard the meat. Return the stock to the pan and reduce to 600ml/1 pint/2½ cups. Cool and store in the refrigerator: when cold it should be a stiff jelly.

3 To make the pastry, place the fats and water in a pan and heat gently to melt – do not boil. Sift the flour and salt into a bowl, make a well in the centre, pour in the liquid and mix. Knead with your hands to form a soft, pliable dough.

4 Roll out three-quarters of the pastry to a circle 8mm/⅓in thick and line a 20cm/8in springform cake tin (pan). Cover the remaining pastry and keep warm.

5 To make the pie filling, combine all the ingredients in a bowl and mix thoroughly using your hands.

6 Spoon the pie filling into the pastry case, gently pushing the mixture into the corners and flattening the top. The meat should come to just below the top of the pastry case. Pre-heat the oven to 180°C/350°F/Gas 4.

7 Roll out the remaining pastry into a circle slightly smaller than the diameter of the pan and lower it on to the meat. Dampen the edge with water, fold over the top of the pastry case and crimp the edges together with your fingertips. Make a 1cm/½in hole in the centre of the lid and brush with the beaten egg.

8 Bake the pie in the preheated oven for 40 minutes to set the pastry, then reduce the heat to 140°C/275°F/Gas 1 and continue to cook for 2 hours. Remove from the oven and leave to cool to room temperature.

9 To finish the pie, warm the jellied stock gently until it is liquid, transfer it to a jug (pitcher) and, using a funnel, carefully pour it into the pie through the hole in the top, a little at a time, until the pie will accept no more.

10 The jelly now needs to set, so refrigerate overnight. Serve the pie cold, or at room temperature, in slices, accompanied by pickles, crisp lettuce and tomatoes.

Energy 728kcal/3045kJ; Protein 42.3g; Carbohydrate 55.7g, of which sugars 1.7g; Fat 38.2g, of which saturates 17.1g; Cholesterol 118mg; Calcium 135mg; Fibre 2.2g; Sodium 215mg

Italian-style Rabbit Casserole

Pulses can bring a warm glow to the soul at any time of the year with their soft textures. Most people are familiar with the dried or canned versions, but summertime brings fresh varieties, which are in a league of their own. Borlotti beans come in pretty white and pink-flecked pods; packed full of protein, carbohydrates and fibre, they are a good meal in themselves. This Italian-based recipe marries the beans with rabbit and the sweet summer flavours of roasted red peppers, basil and Marsala wine.

Serves 6

450g/1lb/3 cups fresh, podded borlotti
   beans (or 225g/8oz/1¼ cups dried
   beans, soaked for 24 hours, or
   2 x 400g/14oz cans beans, drained
   and rinsed)
1 medium-hot red chilli, halved
   lengthways
1 garlic bulb, cut in half horizontally
1 bay leaf
3 large red (bell) peppers
175ml/6fl oz/¾ cup extra virgin
   olive oil
2 rabbits, jointed: hind and front legs
   removed from carcasses, saddles
   cut in half across their length
1 large onion, finely chopped
2 medium carrots, finely diced
2 celery sticks, finely chopped
275ml/9fl oz/1 generous cup
   Marsala wine
600ml/1 pint/2½ cups fresh chicken
   stock (or 1 chicken stock (bouillon)
   cube dissolved in 600ml/1 pint/
   2½ cups water)
24 pitted black olives
24 basil leaves
sea salt and ground black pepper

1 To cook fresh beans, place them in a pan with the chilli, the root half of the garlic, the bay leaf and enough water to cover by 2.5cm/1in. Bring the beans to a simmer and cook gently for 12–15 minutes or until tender.

2 If using dried beans, drain and follow the same procedure but cook for 1 hour, topping up with water when necessary.

3 Meanwhile, char the red peppers on all sides over a gas flame or under a grill (broiler). When the skin is black all over, place the peppers in a bowl and cover with clear film (plastic wrap).

4 Heat the olive oil in a large pan. Season the rabbit joints and fry, turning, to brown all over.

5 Add the onion, carrot and celery to the pan, with the peeled cloves from the top half of the garlic head. Cook very gently for around 10–15 minutes, to soften the vegetables fully and draw out their natural sweetness.

6 Remove the film from the bowl containing the red peppers. The blackened skins will have steamed by now and should be easy to rub off. Remove the stalk, seeds and skin, tear the flesh into strips and reserve with any juices from the bowl.

7 When the vegetables in the pan are soft, add the Marsala wine, bring to the boil and boil vigorously for 1 minute.

8 Add the stock to the pan, season with salt and pepper and bring to a simmer. Partially cover with a lid and simmer on gentle heat for 45 minutes, until the rabbit is tender.

9 Once the rabbit, beans and peppers are all ready, drain the beans, discarding the garlic, chilli and bay leaf, and add to the pan containing the rabbit.

10 Add the peppers, olives and ripped basil leaves, bring back to a simmer, adjust the seasoning and serve.

Energy 720kcal/3016kJ; Protein 54g; Carbohydrate 48g, of which sugars 14.7g; Fat 30.2g, of which saturates 6.3g; Cholesterol 139mg; Calcium 186mg; Fibre 14.3g; Sodium 489mg

Rabbit Salad with Ruby Chard

The saddle is the prime cut of a rabbit, and really the only part of it that can be quickly roasted or fried. If you have a whole rabbit the neck and legs can be used in another recipe, such as a stew or pie, or made in to stock and frozen for the next time you are cooking a game recipe.

3 Make a salad using colourful leaves. Toss with your dressing and place in the centre of four individual plates.

4 Remove the rabbit from the pan and return the pan to the hob, add the butter and, as soon as it is melted, throw the chard in all at once. (It may be heaped up but will soon wilt down.) Season with salt and ground black pepper and toss to coat well with the butter. Once it has wilted – about 3 minutes – it is ready.

5 Slice the rabbit fillets from the back of the saddle and take the small fillets from underneath as well. Cut thinly and strew evenly over the salad. Place the warm chard on top and serve.

Serves 4

15g/1 tbsp groundnut (peanut) oil
2 saddles of rabbit, each weighing
    approximately 250g/9oz
mixed salad leaves
salad dressing
50g/2oz/¼ cup butter
225g/8oz ruby chard leaves (stalks
    removed)
salt and ground black pepper

1 Heat a frying pan and pour in the oil, allowing it to get quite hot. Dry and season the saddles of rabbit and place them skin side down. Reduce the heat and brown lightly in the pan.

2 Turn the saddles over on to the rib side, cover and cook over a very low heat for about 7 minutes. Turn off the heat, and leave to rest.

Variation
You could also make this simple salad with pigeon breasts, and if you can't find chard, young spinach leaves can be substituted.

Energy 287kcal/1192kJ; Protein 29g; Carbohydrate 1g, of which sugars 0.9g; Fat 18.5g, of which saturates 9.1g; Cholesterol 115mg; Calcium 126mg; Fibre 1.2g; Sodium 238mg

Roast Hare with Beetroot

It's not always easy to get hold of hare, but if you can its rich taste goes really well with this beetroot sauce. Venison rump steak can be substituted if you can't find hare, and you could also use rabbit saddles. For a lighter result you could try using yogurt in place of the crème fraîche.

Serves 4

2 saddles of hare
10ml/2 tsp olive oil
350g/12oz cooked beetroot (beets)
30ml/2 tbsp chopped shallot
30ml/2 tbsp white wine vinegar
50g/2oz/¼ cup crème fraîche
5ml/1 tsp English (hot) mustard
salt and ground black pepper

For the marinade
600ml/1 pint/1½ cups red wine
1 carrot, finely diced
1 onion, finely diced
2 sprigs fresh thyme
1 bayleaf
2 sprigs fresh parsley
salt
8 black peppercorns

4 Remove most of the fat from the pan, then add the beetroot. Add the shallot and cook for about 2 minutes to soften. Add the vinegar and 30ml/2 tbsp of the marinade and stir in thoroughly.

5 Simmer the liquid to reduce for 2–3 minutes, stirring, until a coating texture is nearly achieved. Reduce the heat to low and add the crème fraîche. Whisk it in until completely melted, then add the mustard and season to taste. Set aside and keep warm

6 To serve, remove the hare fillets from the top and bottom of the saddles, and slice lengthways.

7 Place on four warmed plates and arrange the beetroot mixture on top. Reheat the sauce, without boiling, and hand round separately.

1 Using a flexible knife, remove the membrane covering the saddles. Mix all the ingredients for the marinade together and coat the saddles, then leave for one day, turning occasionally.

2 Preheat the oven to 240°C/475°F/Gas 9. Take out and dry the saddles with kitchen paper. Strain the marinade through a sieve and set aside

3 Heat the olive oil in a large ovenproof pan. Brown the saddles all over then cook in the preheated oven for 10–15 minutes. They should still be pink. Leave in a warm place to rest.

Classic Jugged Hare

This rich, dark stew of hare is famously finished by the addition of its own blood, and it is best to collect this in the field, directly after the kill. Hang the hare by its hind legs, slit the throat and collect the draining blood in a jar. Once the blood begins to clot, cut the hare down and seal the jar tightly. When you get home, rinse out the stomach cavity with the vinegar in the marinade recipe, reserving the vinegar and any blood clots and adding them to the blood in the jar, which should be refrigerated. The sauce is rich in iron and can be sweetened with redcurrant or crab apple jelly, if you wish.

Serves 4

1 young hare weighing 2kg/4½lb, prepared as above and cut into 10–12 pieces, blood, liver and kidneys reserved
30ml/2 tbsp duck fat or beef dripping
150g/5oz unsmoked streaky (fatty) bacon, diced
50g/2oz/¼ cup butter
1 onion, diced
30ml/2 tbsp plain (all-purpose) flour
600ml/1 pint/2½ cups warm game stock or 1 beef and 1 chicken stock (bouillon) cube dissolved in 600ml/1 pint/2½ cups boiling water
sea salt and ground black pepper

For the marinade
30ml/2 tbsp red wine vinegar
1 onion, cut into 8 pieces
1 large carrot, cut into 8 pieces
1 celery stick, cut into 8 pieces
4 garlic cloves, peeled and halved
2.5ml/½ tsp ground allspice
4 cloves
rind of ½ lemon
1 bay leaf
2 thyme sprigs
10 black peppercorns
1 bottle good red wine or port

1 Mix all the marinade ingredients in a large bowl, and add the jointed hare. Keep in a cool place, overnight, turning two or three times if possible.

2 Drain the meat in a colander. Reserve the liquid and herbs, but discard the vegetables, lemon rind and spices. Pat the meat dry.

3 Season the meat with salt and pepper. Heat a large frying pan or casserole over medium heat, melt the fat or dripping, turn up the heat and fry the seasoned hare until browned all over. Remove from the pan and reserve, covered, in a warm place.

4 Cook the bacon until the fat begins to render and remove this also. Add the butter and cook the onion over more gentle heat, stirring occasionally, until softened and beginning to brown.

5 Add the flour to the pan and stir constantly for a minute or so to cook the flour. Add a ladleful of warm stock and stir until thickened, then repeat this until all the stock has been incorporated.

6 Return the hare and bacon to the pan with the reserved herbs and wine from the marinade.

7 Simmer the hare gently for 1½ hours. If the sauce is a little thin at the end of the cooking time, remove the meat, turn up the heat and reduce the sauce.

8 Wait until you are ready to eat before finishing the dish, as the blood and liver must not be overheated.

9 Just before serving, blitz the liver in a food processor, adding enough of the blood and vinegar mixture to make a smooth paste. Transfer the liver paste to a bowl.

Energy 1001kcal/4191kJ; Protein 116.3g; Carbohydrate 9.8g, of which sugars 2.9g; Fat 55.7g, of which saturates 12.9g; Cholesterol 60mg; Calcium 102mg; Fibre 0.9g; Sodium 713mg

9 ▶ Add a ladleful of hot sauce from the pan to the liver paste, whisking to combine, and then quickly pour the mixture back into the pan, stirring well and heating through, but not allowing the liquid to boil.

10 Serve the jugged hare immediately with heart-shaped croutons (see Cook's tip), boiled potatoes and green beans.

Cook's tip A traditional French garnish for this type of dish is large heart-shaped croutons. You need eight slices of white bread cut into heart shapes. Fry the hearts in goose or duck fat or in clarified butter. When crisp and golden, and still warm, dip the edges of the hearts in very finely chopped parsley.

Game Pâté with Red Onion Marmalade

This country pâté is typical of many found throughout Europe; the blend of coarsely chopped and ground game, bolstered by liver and alcohol, makes a richly satisfying spread. Serve with plenty of crusty bread or toast and sweet-sour onion marmalade to make a perfect lunch to share with friends.

Serves 6–8

350g/12oz boned hare, cut into
  small chunks
115g/4oz boned hare, minced (ground)
  or blitzed in a food processor
the liver from the hare, minced or
  blitzed in a food processor
225g/8oz fatty pork, minced
150ml/¼ pint/⅔ cup Madeira wine
10ml/2 tsp green peppercorns,
  lightly crushed
5ml/1 tsp finely chopped thyme
5ml/1 tsp finely chopped marjoram
12 slices cured ham such as
  prosciutto, Black Forest or Serrano
2 bay leaves
sea salt and ground black pepper

For the red onion marmalade
30ml/2 tbsp olive oil
675g/1½lb red onions, thinly sliced
1 thyme sprig
45ml/3 tbsp balsamic vinegar
10ml/2 tsp caster (superfine) sugar
sea salt and ground black pepper

Variation Almost any game can be substituted for the hare in this recipe; rabbit and pheasant for example. Always include the fatty pork, however, as this is needed for flavour and texture.

1 In a bowl mix the hare meat, minced liver and pork with the wine, green peppercorns, thyme and marjoram. Blend the Madeira into the meat with your hands and leave the mixture in the refrigerator overnight to marinate.

2 Next day, preheat the oven to 160°C/325°F/Gas 3. Line a 600ml/1-pint loaf tin (pan) with ham, arranging four slices along each side and one at each end. Reserve two slices for the top.

3 Re-mix the filling, seasoning with salt and pepper, and spoon it into the tin. Press down and smooth the top.

4 Lay the remaining two slices of ham along the top, then fold the side and end pieces of ham over to encase the filling completely.

5 Place the bay leaves on top and cover with a double layer of foil. Scrunch the foil under the rim of the tin to seal it. Place the tin in an oven tray surrounded by a little water, and bake in the oven for 1½ hours. Remove, cool and refrigerate.

6 To make the onion marmalade, heat a heavy pan over high heat. Add the oil and allow to heat to near smoking before adding the onions. Allow them to sizzle and scorch, then cook vigorously, stirring, for a further 2 minutes. Add the thyme and some seasoning, turn the heat down to low, cover with a lid and simmer for 20 minutes.

7 Once the onions have softened, stir in the vinegar and sugar and cook gently, stirring, until the vinegar has been fully absorbed by the onions. Cool, and then serve with the chilled pâté.

Energy 324kcal/1350kJ; Protein 25g; Carbohydrate 10.6g, of which sugars 8.6g; Fat 18g, of which saturates 4.2g; Cholesterol 28mg; Calcium 38mg; Fibre 1.2g; Sodium 197mg

Squirrel Skewers

Late summer and early autumn mean orchard fruits in abundance, and plump game that has been feeding in readiness for winter. Squirrels don't tend to yield a great deal of meat, but at this time of year they are at their best. This simple appetizer is quickly cooked and therefore utilizes only the loin, which is the prime cut. The plum sauce can be made in bulk, when plums are in season, and frozen.

Serves 2

1 large apple such as Cox, quartered and cored, each piece cut into 3
50g/2oz pork belly, cut into 8 pieces
3 squirrels, cleaned, loins boned out and cut in half lengthways
15ml/1 tbsp olive oil
25g/1oz/2 tbsp butter
2 thyme sprigs
sea salt and ground black pepper
celeriac remoulade, to serve

For the plum dipping sauce
15ml/1 tbsp olive oil
1 whole star anise
5cm/2in cinnamon stick
1 large onion, finely chopped
1kg/2¼lb plums, stoned and diced
75g/3oz soft light brown sugar
100ml/3½fl oz/½ cup sherry vinegar

1 To make the plum sauce, warm a heavy pan over medium heat, add the oil, star anise, cinnamon stick and onion and cook for 5–8 minutes, stirring occasionally, until the onion is soft.

2 Stir in the plums, sugar and sherry vinegar, bring to a simmer and cook on low heat, uncovered, stirring occasionally, for 30 minutes.

3 When the plums have broken down and the sauce has thickened, allow it to cool before using or freezing.

4 Take four 15cm/6in skewers. Spear a piece of apple, then pork, then squirrel, apple, squirrel, pork and apple on to each skewer. Season.

5 Warm a griddle or frying pan over medium heat and add the oil, then the butter. When the butter foams, add the kebabs, with the thyme, and cook for 3–4 minutes. Turn the skewers through 90 degrees and cook for a further 3 minutes. Repeat on all sides and remove from the pan to rest before serving with the plum sauce.

Cook's tip Make a celeriac remoulade to accompany this dish. Peel and grate a small celeriac, mix with mayonnaise and crème fraîche to moisten and add 2 chopped shallots, 2 chopped gherkins, 15ml/1 tsp chopped capers and 5ml/1 tsp English mustard powder.

Energy 881kcal/3700kJ; Protein 55.9g; Carbohydrate 84.5g, of which sugars 84.3g; Fat 37.9g, of which saturates 13.8g; Cholesterol 144mg; Calcium 110mg; Fibre 8.2g; Sodium 287mg

Fricassée of Squirrel and Mustard

When planning to hunt squirrel for the pot, try to bag the younger ones. As with most game, the older the animal the tougher the meat. If you do end up with older meat, soak it in salted water for 4–6 hours. Acorns have a high level of bitter tannins and the salt will help to draw these out. Cooked in sweet white wine and finished with crème fraîche, this recipe has quite an elegant finish.

Serves 4

2 squirrels, jointed, hind legs split,
   saddle cut in 2, fore legs removed
50g/2oz well-seasoned plain
   (all-purpose) flour
30ml/2 tbsp olive oil
50g/2oz/¼ cup butter
16 button (pearl) onions, peeled
8 garlic cloves, peeled
300ml/½ pint/1¼ cups Sauternes or a
   similar sweet dessert wine
300ml/½ pint/1¼ cups chicken stock
   or 1 chicken stock (bouillon) cube
   dissolved in hot water
150ml/¼ pint/⅔ cup crème fraîche
15ml/1 tbsp Dijon mustard
20 tarragon leaves
sea salt and ground black pepper
bread or mashed potatoes, to serve

**For the sautéed courgettes
   and almonds**
75g/3oz/6 tbsp butter
600g/1lb 6oz courgettes (zucchini),
   cut into 6mm/⅓in slices
50g/2oz slivered almonds, toasted
1 bunch dill, roughly chopped
sea salt and ground black pepper

1 Dredge the squirrel in seasoned flour. Heat a large pan and add the oil, then the butter and when it foams add the squirrel and fry gently, turning frequently, for 20 minutes. Add the onions and continue cooking for 5 minutes. Add the garlic and cook for a further 5 minutes.

2 Add the wine, stock and some seasoning. Bring gently to a simmer, cover the pan and cook over very low heat for 1¼ hours.

3 Meanwhile, to make the sautéed courgettes, preheat the oven to 200°C/400°F/Gas 6. Heat a large frying pan, add a third of the butter, allow to sizzle and add a third of the sliced courgettes. Season and fry for 2 minutes, turning the courgettes, then transfer to an ovenproof dish.

4 Cook the remaining courgettes in the same way in two further batches. Add the almonds and dill to the baking dish and stir them in, then bake in the hot oven for 5 minutes.

5 Remove the lid of the rabbit pan and simmer until the liquid has reduced so it just covers the bottom of the pan.

6 Stir in the crème fraîche, mustard and tarragon and warm the sauce gently. Serve with the courgettes and some fresh bread or mashed potatoes.

Energy 698kcal/2896kJ; Protein 24.6g; Carbohydrate 22.6g, of which sugars 11.4g; Fat 51.2g, of which saturates 26g; Cholesterol 132mg; Calcium 141mg; Fibre 3.4g; Sodium 265mg

Index

bacon
Brussels sprouts with bacon 44–5
classic jugged hare 80–1
daube of venison 66–7
Polish hunter's stew 82–3
wild boar hock with buckwheat dumplings 72–3
beans
cassoulet-style duck confit and beans 34–5
Italian-style rabbit casserole 88–9
pot-roast partridge with grapes and sherry 110
southern fried turkey and succotash 50–1
sticky wild boar ribs with Boston baked beans 70–1
venison chilli con carne 62–3
boar
slow-roast belly of wild boar 68
sticky wild boar ribs with Boston baked beans 70–1
wild boar hock with buckwheat dumplings 72–3
wild boar, chickpea, saffron and pepper stew 69
braised shoulder of goat with anchovy 76
Brussels sprouts with bacon 44–5
buckwheat
wild boar hock with buckwheat dumplings 72–3

casserole of goat with lettuce and peas 78–9
cassoulet-style duck confit and beans 34–5
chunky goat moussaka 77
classic jugged hare 90–1
classic roast woodcock with fried bread, game chips and watercress 18–19
courgette gratin 66–7
courgettes and almonds 95
crispy tarragon pheasant 41
crofter's pie 74–5

daube of venison 66–7
duck
cassoulet-style duck confit and beans 34–5
roast duck with orange and Drambuie 38–9
sautéed duck breast with Jansson's temptation 36–7
fricassée of squirrel and mustard 95

game pâté with red onion marmalade 92–3

German-style roast goose 44–5
goat
braised shoulder of goat with anchovy 76
casserole of goat with lettuce and peas 78–9
chunky goat moussaka 77
crofter's pie 74–5
goose
German-style roast goose 44–5
goose hash with fried egg and mustard sauce 46–7
rillette of goose 48–9
grouse
grouse baked in heather 22–3
pot-roast grouse with polenta 20–1
guinea fowl
guinea fowl Normandine 28
guinea fowl with lemon balm and mint butter 29

hare
classic jugged hare 90–1
game pâté with red onion marmalade 92–3

Italian-style rabbit casserole 88–9

jugged hare 90–1

Moroccan pigeon pie 14–15

Norfolk pheasant pasty 42–3

pan haggerty 70
pan-fried pigeon and pease pudding 10–11
partridge
pot-roast partridge with grapes and sherry 32–3
rabbit and game pie 86–7
roast partridge with caramelized pears 30–1
pheasant
crispy tarragon pheasant 41
Norfolk pheasant pasty 42–3
Polish hunter's stew 82–3

Umbrian roast pheasant with spinach salad 40
pigeon terrine with spiced apricot chutney 12–13
plum dipping sauce 94
polenta
pot-roast grouse with polenta 20–1
Polish hunter's stew 82–3
pot-roast grouse with polenta 20–1
pot-roast partridge with grapes and sherry 32–3
potatoes
clapshot potatoes 30–1
classic roast woodcock with fried bread, game chips and watercress 18–19
colcannon 58
crofter's pie 74–5
German-style roast goose 44–5
potato dumplings 72, 82–3
roast haunch of roe deer 56–7
roast teal with green peppercorn sauce and apple rösti 8–9
salad of quail and truffle oil 26
Salardaise potatoes 24–5
sautéed duck breast with Jansson's temptation 36–7
venison steak with all the trimmings 64–5
potted rabbit 84–5

quail
salad of quail and truffle oil 26
salmis of quail 24–5

rabbit
Italian-style rabbit casserole 88–9
Polish hunter's stew 82–3
potted rabbit 84–5
rabbit and game pie 86–7
rillette of goose 48–9
roast duck with orange and Drambuie 38–9
roast partridge with caramelized pears 108
roast teal with green peppercorn sauce and apple rösti 8–9
roast woodcock salad with gooseberry relish 16–17
rouille 69

salad of quail and truffle oil 26–7
salmis of quail 24–5
sautéed duck breast with Jansson's temptation 36–7
seared venison carpaccio 59
slow-roast belly of wild boar 68
southern fried turkey and succotash 50–1

squirrel
fricassée of squirrel and mustard 95
squirrel skewers 94
sticky wild boar ribs with Boston baked beans 70

teal
roast teal with green peppercorn sauce and apple rösti 8–9
turkey
southern fried turkey and succotash 50–1
turkey schnitzel, spätzle and pickled mushrooms 52–3

Umbrian roast pheasant 40

venison
daube of venison 66–7
roast haunch of roe deer 65–7
seared venison carpaccio 59
venison agrodolce 60–1
venison chilli con carne 62–3
venison heart braised in Guinness 58
venison steak with all the trimmings 64–5

wild boar hock with buckwheat dumplings 72–3
wild boar, chickpea, saffron and pepper stew 69
wood pigeon
Moroccan pigeon pie 14–15
pan-fried pigeon and pease pudding 10–11
pigeon terrine with spiced apricot chutney 12–13
Polish hunter's stew 82–3
woodcock
classic roast woodcock with fried bread, game chips and watercress 18–19
roast woodcock salad with gooseberry relish 16–17